Finish the Race

D0827422

Finish the Race

Eric Liddell

John W. Keddie

CF4•K

10 9 8 7 6 5 4

Copyright © 2011 John W. Keddie

Paperback ISBN: 978-1-84550-590-5

epub ISBN: 978-1-84550-877-7

mobi ISBN: 978-1-84550-878-4

Reprinted 2012, 2014, 2016

Published by
Christian Focus Publications,
Geanies House, Fearn, Ross-shire,
IV20 1TW, Scotland, U.K.
Tel: +44 (0)1862 871011; Fax: +44 (0)1862 871699
www.christianfocus.com
e-mail: info@christianfocus.com

Cover design by Daniel van Straaten
Illustrated by Brent Donoho
Printed and bound by Nørhaven, Denmark

Scripture quotations are based on the King James Version
of the Bible.

Contents

Paris 1924

It was a really hot day, that Friday. There was a heat wave in Paris during the Olympic Games in the July of 1924 when the sporting world descended on France for the Games of the 8th Olympiad. Friday, 11th July was another day of finals in the Olympic Stadium at Colombes. The 400 metres was scheduled for 6.30 in the evening, so it was just a little cooler than it had been two-and-three-quarter hours earlier when the semi-finals had been run off.

It was now half past six on the dot and the 400 metre finalists were at the starting point.

The crowd and the athletes had just been treated to 'Scotland the Brave!' by a band of the Queen's Own Cameron Highlanders. It was designed to encourage the lone Scot among the finalists.

But the finalists had come to the final challenge. At stake, an Olympic gold medal for one of them.

There were six lanes on the track. They were distinguished by white markings and strings down the two long straights. Because the race was run in lanes, the runners did not start on the same line across the track. There was a 'staggered' start, so that each successive athlete in each lane towards the outside

7

started a few yards in front of the man in the lane inside him. The athletes – the best in the world in the event – had a long back straight, a long bend and a long home straight to negotiate.

'À vous marques!' the starter's voice boomed out.

Two Americans, two Britons, a Swiss and a Canadian moved forward to the start line of their lane. On the cinder track they had dug little holes for their feet to be placed in. Then they crouched down for the next of the starter's orders.

The crowd was silent. You could hear a pin drop. You could almost feel the tension as the athletes and the crowd waited for the crack of the starter's pistol. Most of the spectators were in the stand on the other side of the track, where the race would finish.

On the very outside lane was one of the British athletes. Eric Liddell was a Scot. He was one of the very select band of Scottish track athletes who had reached an Olympic final. In the past four years he had been one of the top British sprinters at shorter distances. Now he was in an event he had only taken up seriously in the past year. And yet, here he was in an Olympic final! He was a bit of a 'dark horse'. After a great win in his semi-final just over two-and-a-half hours earlier, he was now up against some experienced quarter-milers. He was running in a lane where the other athletes could keep their eye on him, but he had no view of them!

Eric settled in to his starting position. He lifted his eyes and looked up the track. It was a long straight before they would reach the bend. How would he run the race? He'd had so little experience before the Games. But he had received great help from Tom McKerchar, a well-known athletics coach in Edinburgh. Tom had trained him more or less from the start of his running at Edinburgh University where Eric had been a student since 1920. Eric remembered the tough running schedules which Tom had put him through, especially over the past winter. Blood, sweat and tears. But it had worked. At least here he was in an Olympic final. Who would have thought it? A China-born son of Scottish missionary parents. Happily, Tom was in the crowd. Sadly, none of Eric's family was.

It was a strange providence that brought him to this moment. In a way, it was because he was a committed and devout Christian. He had been expected to compete in the 'blue ribbon' event of the Games – the 100 metres. Trouble was, that would have involved competition on a Sunday. For Eric, Sunday was the Lord's Day, a day for rest and worship. It was not for work and sport. He wouldn't be running in Sunday events. It was his principle as a Christian that the fourth commandment required one day of rest in seven and the Christian's day of rest and worship, since the rising of Jesus from the dead, was the first day of the week. That was the Christian Sabbath. No, he wouldn't be running on God's day. Still, there were two events which would not involve Sunday races – the 200 metres and 400 metres. So, when he knew the 100 metres was out, he would concentrate on these events. But he had no idea how he would compete against the best in the world in them. As it turned out, he had done well in the 200 metres. A couple of days earlier (9th July) he had actually won a bronze medal behind two top American athletes. It had been a great performance.

People admired Eric's stand for the Lord's Day. And Eric was not slow to make clear his love for the Lord's Day and the day's Lord. In fact just before the final, a team physio had passed him a note. Eric said he would read it at the Stadium. When he opened it up he read:

> *In the old book it says, 'He who honours me I will honour'.*
> *Wishing you the best of success always.*

That note encouraged him. It contained a quote from the Bible, from 1 Samuel 2:30 ('those who honour me, I will honour').

The fact that someone understood his stand and sympathised with him gave him a great lift. He thanked God and took courage. He did trust in the Lord Jesus. Not that he would win the race, but that the Lord would enable him to acquit himself in a way which would honour his Master.

'Prêts!' boomed the starter.

The athletes uniformly rose to a 'set' position. They were like coiled up springs waiting for the report of the gun. At that moment, time seemed to stand still. Eric's heart was pounding and all his faculties were on edge. The question was still going round in Eric's mind: 'How will I run this race?' He still felt a degree of tiredness in his legs and lungs after winning his semi-final less than three hours before, in a personal best performance – 48.2 seconds – only a few tenths of a second behind world record time. Would he last the pace in the final? Would the others just sweep through on the inside, down the home straight? How would he run the race? But time was up for thinking of that …

Early Years

Although he was popularly known as the 'Flying Scot,' Eric had in fact been born in China.

He had come into the world in the city of Tientsin in North China on 16th January, 1902. Naturally he didn't know much about that. Which was probably just as well, given that these were days of great social and political upheaval in China. He was the second son of Christian missionary parents. His father had been appointed as missionary by the London Missionary Society (LMS) in 1898 to Mongolia, an area north of China bordering on Russia. The following year, Eric's father had married Eric's mother in Shanghai. But things were tough for Christian missionaries at that time.

A month after Eric's parents' wedding there was an uprising among a society known as the 'Boxers'. These were very patriotic Chinese who wished to maintain the distinctly Chinese traditions and lifestyle. They were part of the Imperial Army of the Empress-Dowager Tzu-Hsi and late in 1899 she started what became a slogan for the Boxers:

'Kill the foreigners, kill the foreigners, kill them before breakfast.'

This was frightening for foreigners, needless to say. The aim of the Government, aided by Boxer forces, was to wipe out all trace of the Christian religion from the land. Christianity was seen as particularly threatening to the Chinese culture. The Boxers were ruthless, cruelly killing men, women and children. They were fanatical about ancient Chinese culture and martial arts, which is why they were commonly known as 'the society of harmonious fists!' Many Protestant missionaries were killed in the period of the Boxers' activities from November 1899 to September 1901.

At the time of the Boxer Rebellion, James and Mary Liddell were at Ch'ao Yang in Manchuria, North China. They were staying with LMS doctor, Tom Cochrane, a Scotsman from Greenock, and his wife, Grace, with their three children. James took on the Church-based side of the work there. When stories filtered through early in 1900 of atrocities committed by the Boxers nearby, they realised that they would have to flee for their lives.

'Look,' said Tom, 'you all must get away from here. Go to the railhead with James. It's sixty miles away. You'll be able to get to safety from there. James can return to the mission and we'll get away somehow.'

So James took Grace Cochrane and her three young children, with his wife, Mary, and set off for the nearest railhead. They faced considerable dangers on their way, but they reached their destination safely enough.

Meantime, in view of the dangerous situation he faced, Tom Cochrane decided to make a dash for the railhead in the hope of reaching his family. He dressed in Chinese clothes and went on horseback, facing terrible danger. Eventually he met up with them.

'Tom, I wasn't going to move till you came.' Grace Cochrane had refused to go on in the hope that her husband would join them.

The group of Christian missionaries were thankful to the Lord for being kept safe thus far and they duly boarded the next train for Shanghai and relative safety.

It wasn't long before Mary gave birth to their first child, a son whom they named Robert Victor. That was in August 1900 at the London Missionary Society compound in Shanghai.

A few months later, however, the intrepid James and Mary returned to the north, to be settled in Tientsin. From there, James took a trip into Mongolia to see what had happened to the Chinese Christians there. He toured the area for four months or so, accompanied by 200 soldiers!

Sixteen months after Robert came into the world, Eric was born at Tientsin. He was baptised Eric Henry Liddell. Originally, his parents intended him to be called Henry Eric.

On the way to the baptism someone said:

'What is his name?'

'Henry Eric,' said the young child's father.

'Maybe 'Eric Henry' would be better, don't you think? After all, think of how the initials would run together!'

Eric Henry it became.

A daughter was born into the family circle late in 1903. She was named Janet Lillian, though she was always known as Jenny. She was also born in Tientsin. By that time, the family was settled about 180 miles to the south west of Tientsin in a place called Siaochang. This was on the great plain of North China, a plain with thousands of villages – 'As close to one another as currents in a rich cake,' was how someone put it.

The plain contained millions of people. But that's where James and Mary were to serve the Lord, and that's where Eric and his older brother spent the first few years of their life.

Unlike their sister, Jenny, the boys would be left in Britain for their education after the Liddells' first home leave in 1907–08 (this leave is usually called a 'furlough'). Every seven years or so missionaries had an extended break at 'home' – usually a year. This was the 'home leave'.

Apart from visits home to Britain with her parents, Jenny remained in China until she finally came back with them in 1929, when her father retired from missionary service. The same was true of the fourth child of the Liddell home, Ernest Blair, who was born in Peking (Beijing) in December 1912.

Rob and Eric first went back to Britain with their parents and Jenny, in 1907. They did have some memories of the early days in China. Eric didn't remember much of it. He vaguely remembered the mission compound at Siaochang to where his father had been posted when work in Mongolia did not open up. Eric's sister later described the set-up:

'The LMS station in Siaochang consisted then of four large houses in a row. They had verandas on two sides, both upstairs and down. Behind the houses were the Church, a Boys' School and a Girls' School. These were surrounded by a high wall built of mud, with a large gate closed at night.'

Eric remembered the freedom of the compound, playing games with Rob and the Chinese children. It was very hot and dusty in the summer. He remembered chasing round the dining room, the kittens that had been brought from Tientsin. The first phrase he had learned in Chinese was 'Hsieo mao pao la' ('Little cat has run away'). And he had to wear a wadded Chinese coat and a big wide-brimmed hat to keep off the sun. The boys had a Chinese *amah* who cared for them while their mother cared for the patients in the hospital.

The Mission Societies had a retreat on the Po Hai coast at Pei-tai-ho. Eric loved it, as did the other children, playing so much in the sea and on the sandy beaches. He also remembered the quiet Sundays, the Church services and family worship times. These made a distinct impression that was to remain with him for his whole life. Christ was the centre of the home. He remembered during the hymn-singing times how he had always requested the 'Ninety and Nine,' but always cried when it came to the sad bit, about the sheep that was lost and alone on the mountains. Above all, it was the lovely Christian atmosphere of the home from his earliest days that Eric most warmly remembered. Perhaps he knew nothing else and took it for granted. But it all flooded back when he later came to commit himself personally to the Lord some years later.

Family Roots

Eric's father, James Dunlop Liddell, had been born into a Christian home in Greenock in September 1870. He had four sisters, three older and one younger. His father, Robert, Eric's father's father, came from the Stirlingshire village of Killearn. He married Elizabeth Strachan in Greenock in 1859. He had gone to Greenock to work as a joiner, and all five of their children were born there. Sadly, Elizabeth died shortly after the birth of the youngest daughter in 1873. The Liddells didn't stay long in Greenock after that. Robert took his family to Drymen, not far from his native village in Stirlingshire, in the mid 1870s.

The family had been 'Evangelical Union,' an Independent Scottish Church which was later to unite with the Congregational Church. In Drymen, however, where Robert became a grocer, there was no EU Church, and the family attached themselves to the United Presbyterian Church in the village. The family religion was one of a simple gospel in which there was a concern to be faithful to Jesus Christ and witness for him.

Drymen was a lovely picturesque village set among wooded hills, lochs and wonderful sunrises and sunsets – that is, when the skies were clear! A pleasant place in which to live. And it was there that Eric's father grew up and was schooled. When it came to work, in the late 1880s, he took an apprenticeship with a firm of drapers in nearby Stirling, to where he had to move. He was never to follow that as a trade, however, because he would come to believe that the Lord was calling him to serve as a missionary.

In Stirling, James sat under the ministry of the Rev William Blair in the Congregational Church. He came to profess faith in Christ and he entered the membership of the Church there. It was under Blair's ministry that James felt a call to enter Christian work.

'Mr Blair, I feel the Lord is calling me into his service as a missionary.'

'You must make this a matter of prayer, James, and if the Lord is laying this upon your heart apply for acceptance by the Church and take the training they set for you.'

In 1894 James duly went up to the Evangelical Union Theological Hall in Glasgow. So deep an influence did William Blair have on Eric's father's Christian life that he called his youngest son Ernest Blair after his early spiritual mentor.

But it takes two to make the family. Eric's mother, had also been brought up in a Christian home. Her name was Mary Reddin and she was from the village of Paxton near Berwick in the Scottish borders. Like Drymen, where James Liddell was brought up, the area in which Mary grew up was picturesque, set amidst rolling hills, streams and lush farming land. Her father, Henry, was the local blacksmith who had plenty work to do for the farming community around.

Henry Reddin married Janet Mabon in 1857 and Mary was the middle one of their five children. She had two brothers and two sisters. Mary had been born in October 1870. In due time, Henry felt the call of the Lord into Christian work and in the 1880s he upped sticks and moved to Glasgow to work there as a colporteur. This involved going round with Bibles and gospel portions and tracts, encouraging people to be converted to Jesus.

The family attended the Elgin Street Congregational Church in the city. Actually, it was on the corner of the street they lived on!

James and Mary first met in 1893. It was at a congregational outing of the Elgin Street congregation to Stirling. Mary and James hit it off. James moved to the theological hall in Glasgow the following year. Though he was not a member of the same congregation as Mary, for part of his training he did mission work with the congregation of which Mary was a member.

Their friendship soon developed into love with a view to marriage. James, however, still had his training to finish. And Mary, having for some years been a 'tea saleswoman,' went into nursing which for a year or so took her to the Island of Lewis in the Western Isles, off the North-west of Scotland.

James Liddell was a typical Victorian. Though prematurely bald, he always sported a bushy moustache. Mary was a young woman of striking good looks, who wore long, flowing dresses and kept her hair up in the fashion of the day, something she maintained throughout her life. Though never 'well off', Mary was never anything less than elegant in her appearance.

Most important for James and Mary was the common love they had for Jesus and for Christian mission work. James applied for service in the London Missionary Society after he graduated from the theological hall. In 1898 he was sent to Mongolia to succeed the Rev John Parker who had followed the famous Scottish missionary James Gilmour (1843–1891) in the work. Mary was to join James a year later.

In their early married life James and Mary had to endure the hardships of the exciting and dangerous days of the Boxer uprising and the years that followed in the building up of the missionary work in North China. Following the Lord in his service may be hard and costly, but it is always rewarding. As far as family life was concerned, in spring 1907 the Liddells took their first break and father, mother, Rob, Eric and young Jenny, took the long journey by sea back 'home' for their first home leave. There would be no return trip for the boys for many years.

School Days

School days are happy days. So it has been said, though perhaps that wasn't everyone's experience.

They were for Eric, though not right at the start. Eric first landed on British shores with his family early in 1907. They travelled to Scotland and initially had a wonderful time doing the rounds of the relatives in Glasgow and Drymen and enjoying the beautiful countryside or busy city life.

During the time at home, however, James Liddell also had many speaking engagements in churches and Christian missionary meetings on behalf of the London Missionary Society (LMS) work in which he was engaged.

Eric couldn't help noticing that though it was high summer in Scotland it was a whole lot cooler than what he had known in China. But it was all so lush and green, with a wonderful variety of deciduous and coniferous trees breaking up the landscape. Drymen, where Grandfather Liddell and Eric's aunts lived, was set amidst some of the prettiest scenery in Scotland. It was strange, too, not to see any Chinese faces. And the dress was so different. Indeed, everything was so different in the 'homeland' – the sights and smells and sounds and social life.

The question of the boys' education concerned Eric's parents. If they were to be schooled in the United Kingdom this would mean separation from parents and siblings for around seven years. That would be a wrench both for parents and children. However, after much prayer to the Lord for guidance James and Mary decided that it would be for the best for Rob and Eric to be educated in England.

The education of missionaries' children was a common issue in those days. The churches and missionary agencies were fully conscious of this and as early as 1842 the London Missionary Society, for which James worked, had established a Boys' Mission School at Walthamstow in Essex.

The school was called 'The Old Barn'. It was a building of four stories with a playground about perhaps one hundred feet by one hundred feet. It appears that the accommodation was always on the tight side, with long, stone corridors, and, besides the classrooms, two large dormitories and four or five small ones for all the boys' accommodation. It was after all a 'home' as well as a school. The windows were small and so the light in the school was limited. The playground was an asphalted square, though big enough for various games, including 'touch rugby'. It was very tight.

In September 1908, James and Mary Liddell registered Rob and Eric at the School for the Sons of Missionaries (SSM) in Blackheath. Their father immediately left for the Far East, though mother and Jenny stayed on for a year, most of the time living near the school. The time came, however, for Mrs Liddell and Jenny to travel back to China. That was in September 1909.

'Boys, make sure you write to me every week, now.'

'Yes, ma,' they replied, hardly knowing what they were saying. However, that letter-writing would become very precious both for Rob and Eric – and for Mary and James Liddell.

Mary's last glimpse of the boys was from the road looking down on the playground. They were engrossed in a game of cricket and didn't even notice her! Maybe it was best that way. But it would be over four years before they would meet again. That night, when Eric realised his mother and sister had gone to join his dad, he cried himself to sleep. He was only seven.

It was a great blessing, though, for Eric to have Rob with him at the school. The boys were very close and in his school days, especially in the early years, Eric leant quite a bit for support on his older brother. Eric always had the reputation as a quiet chap, and very friendly. Though there was occasional bullying and coarseness, the company at school was congenial. After all, many of the boys were from Christian missionary families and had much the same background and influences as the Liddell boys.

The discipline in the school, too, was strict, but fair under a strong headmaster, Mr W. B. Hayward.

The education was sound and, as was often the case in such boarding schools, there was a fair emphasis on sports and games. Mind you, the school in those days at Blackheath didn't have a sports field of its own. For its rugby and cricket, as well as the athletics, it used the heath near the school, though from time to time it also rented other sports parks and fields nearby as necessity or opportunity arose.

As a school for the sons of missionaries, run by Missionary Societies, there was within it, also, a strong influence of Christian faith. The school at Blackheath was right next to the Blackheath Congregational Church, to which Rob and Eric Liddell went for worship services on Sunday. The Baptist boys, however, would have a half hour walk to the nearest Baptist Church. The spiritual influences were clearly very profound as in the course of the years many of the boys who passed through the school at Blackheath – including Rob and Eric Liddell – went on to missionary service. Put it this way, the school presented no discouragement to such Christian service, quite the contrary.

Because of the rather tight accommodation and lack of playing fields the school was always on the lookout for a new location. Opportunity presented itself in 1912, when the former Royal Navy School and grounds at Mottingham in Kent became available and were purchased. The building had originally been known as Fairy Hill and it became in 1912 Eltham

College, Eltham being the area in which the college was located. So, in January 1912, seventy-three boys with all the masters moved to the new college at Eltham.

This opened up new opportunities for education and sport, as for the first time the college had a sports field of its own. There was also a lot more space within the college, as well as a college chapel for worship services.

This was 'home' for the Liddell boys, as well as all the other boarders. They were well cared for and obviously the experience tended to instil independence and discipline. Though separated from parents, the boys wrote to them every single week. This meant that they constantly thought on their family ties and gave their own news, and received news from parents. Obviously it took time for correspondence to travel in those days. Nevertheless it was good to stay in touch though in fact they were so far away.

Eric's parents with Jenny and new little brother, Ernest, who was just one year old at the time, returned on a home leave at the beginning of 1914. Naturally again holidays were spent with the family in Scotland. By the time Rob and Eric's parents came to return to China in March 1915, the Great War had broken out. These were days of terrible uncertainties.

In 1917, Rob and Eric both came into the membership of the local Congregational Church in Eltham. They were, of course, very attentive at worship, Bible classes and Christian meetings. The early Christian influences of home, school and church impressed upon Eric's heart and mind, respect both for the Christian faith and the Christian Sabbath.

Eric, like his brother, Rob, was always a good scholar. One master was to say of him that he was 'one of the less boisterous members of his form'. Of course he had the example of a fine older brother. Rob was highly thought of, and in a way a hard act for Eric to follow.

Eric also excelled at rugby and cricket in the college, and was rugby captain 1918–20, cricket captain 1918–20, and winner of the Blackheath Cup in 1918. Besides this he set many college track records, one of which – 10.2 seconds for the 100 yards, set in 1919 – was not improved on for forty years!

In the autumn of 1919, Rob went up to Edinburgh University to study medicine, a five-year course. Eric, therefore, had a year at Eltham without his brother. He was one of the outstanding students in the College that year. He also determined to go up to Edinburgh University.

'Liddell, you'll need French to get into University. You'll have to do it in the summer.'

In the summer of 1920 Eric duly took French and he finally 'matriculated' as they call it at Edinburgh University for a Bachelor of Science degree in February 1921.

Scholar and Sportsman

'Weren't you good at the sprints in school, Eric?'

'Well, I did set the college record for the 100, a couple of years ago. But really, I don't have the time for it. I've too much class work to get on with.'

'Pity,' said his enthusiastic friend.

In the spring of 1920, Eric and Rob had the joy of a reunion with their mother, sister, and younger brother, Ernest, who had come home rather earlier than expected, in advance of their father. Their father returned in his regular home leave in May 1921. What happy times they had as a family that summer! But something else happened in Eric's life that spring. Since leaving college early in 1920, Eric hadn't taken part in any sport seriously. But early in 1921, a friend invited him to do some training for the forthcoming Edinburgh University Sports.

'What's all this about work and no time for recreation?' he reflected when he thought about the invitation to take up athletics again.

The conviction dawned on him that it would be good to get out into the open air and get into sports once more. He would, after all, take up his friend's challenge and train for the University Sports to be held at the end of May at Craiglockhart. That wasn't far away. However, he'd already agreed to a cycling holiday with friends to Fort William, to climb Scotland's highest peak, Ben Nevis, and that was just three or four weeks before the Sports.

'Not a good idea,' said his friend, 'not good for training.'

Eric didn't pay any heed and went off on his trip. On returning, however, he found that his 'novice' friend had been right. His muscles had no spring. Still, he set-to the practice. Not that that amounted to much. So, it was a very inexperienced and rather untrained young sprinter who turned up at the University Sports for his first public appearance.

But what an appearance it was! In a 100 yards heat he really pushed the experienced Innes Stewart. In the final, he went one better with a great win. A new force had arrived in university athletics!

Eric never looked back. Within a month he was double Scottish sprint champion –100 and 220 yards. He also had his first taste of international competition. It was in a Triangular International in Belfast in July. This involved the home nations: Scotland, England (and Wales), and Ireland. He won the 100 yards that day, defeating the best of the home countries' sprinters and in the process put down a marker that a real sprinting talent had emerged in Scotland.

By this time Eric had been taken under the wing of a fine Edinburgh trainer, Tom McKerchar, the official starter for the Edinburgh University Sports. For the next four years, till Eric departed for China in July 1925, Tom was to put him through his paces.

'Come on, Eric, you've got to be quicker off your mark. Do that start again! ... Keep on your toes. ... Make sure you stretch your muscles and keep warm before the races.'

Tom never tried to change the young sprinter's style, but he did successfully harness his raw power and determination to win. Not that Eric had an exceptional build. At his peak, he stood a mere five feet nine inches and weighed around eleven stones. But he had great heart and he put a lot into the training that Tom set for him. And he put a lot into his races.

Many of the track meets then involved what were called 'handicap' races. This meant that the athletes with good form were put on a back mark, running the full distance, whereas those who were thought to be lesser athletes were given various starts, sometimes up to as much as eighteen yards in a 100 yards race. This meant that runners like Eric had to run flat out all the time. It was great competition for bringing the best out of the quicker men.

It wasn't that Eric spent much time in training. Eric was down at the track near Leith only two or three times a week for practice. But he certainly blossomed under Tom's training routine.

By the end of the 1921 season, one major daily newspaper in Scotland, *The Glasgow Herald*, even predicted that it wouldn't be long before he was a British champion sprinter, and might even develop into an Olympic hero. Even by the end of that first season, as a nineteen-year-old, he was sweeping all before him on the Scottish tracks.

A track star had emerged. But Eric's studies didn't suffer. He was doing a pure science degree, and in his first year actually achieved great results in his exams. In everything he was involved in, he showed tremendous determination and did not shirk hard work.

While in Edinburgh, Eric went to Morningside Congregational Church at what was commonly called Holy Corner. It was called that because it was at a junction where there were church buildings at all four corners!

Every Lord's Day the Liddell family, (Rob, Eric and the others if they were home) would take their places in the congregation. The boys had professed faith in the local Congregational Church at Eltham a few years earlier and had always been taught to respect the Lord's Day. The day was for rest and worship, and certainly not for organised sports or recreations.

Whilst respectful for all that was Christian, Eric was quiet about matters of Christian faith in the early years at university. He was a bit of a 'secret disciple'. At the same time he was never taken up with the 'social life' of the students. He was certainly never a smoker or alcohol drinker. In that area, he followed a very strong family temperance tradition.

After his successful track season, it stood to reason that someone would enquire whether he might have been a rugger man at college:

'I say, Liddell, did you play any rugby at school?'

'Well, yes, I did; I played on the wing.'

'Great, come along to join the University Rugby Club when we start up in September, won't you?'

In fact, brother Rob was already a member of the University rugby first fifteen and when Eric joined the club for the 1921–22 season they made a very effective wing partnership – Rob a centre three quarter to Eric's wing three-quarter.

It was soon clear that with his speed, Eric would be a powerful asset for the rugby team. Representative matches soon followed. Chosen for the Edinburgh-Glasgow Inter-City match and International trials, Eric was soon elevated to the Scotland International team, playing for Scotland for the first time in the 3-3 draw against France in Paris on 2nd January, 1922.

Eric was a great 'find' for the International team, as he proved over the seven international matches he played in the 1921–22 and 1922–23 seasons. And it wasn't that he was just a sprinter. He was good in defence too. His pace, however, was explosive and with another former Eltham College old boy, A. L. Gracie, who was his centre, he put fear into many an opposition, not least on the international stage.

Track Champion and Evangelist

In the years he competed on the track in the United Kingdom, Eric Liddell was a very active and consistent performer. In scratch races – Edinburgh University Sports, Inter-University Championships and Scottish Championships – he ruled the roost, completely dominating the events.

In the 1922 season, he started with a bang at his own University Sports by setting a Scottish Native record in the 220 yards with 21.8, the first time a Scot had been under 22 seconds in Scotland.

A measure of Eric's improvement that year was clear to see in the last track meeting of the season, at the Celtic Football Club Sports in August. The meetings of the big soccer clubs were among the most important of the athletics' calendar. Sometimes there were as many as 800 entrants to these football club annual sports. Most events were 'handicap' events, in which the better runners gave starts to the lesser. But sometimes they were 'scratch' races, all invited athletes running the full distance.

That August at Parkhead, in an Invitation 120 yards race, Eric was matched, with others, against possibly the best sprinter in Britain of the time, Harry Edward.

Edward had won bronze medals in the 100 metres and 200 metres at the Olympic Games of 1920 at Antwerp. At Celtic Park, though, the young Scot had a great win over the seasoned sprinter.

The year 1923 was crucial for Eric in more ways than one. There had been a change in his life in relation to Jesus Christ and Christian faith. The decisive change came when he met with a young divinity student at Glasgow, who was actively involved in evangelism. The name of that divinity student was David Patrick Thomson, better known even then as 'D.P.' D.P. with other students, including Eric's brother, Rob, in the spring of 1923, were involved in mission work at a place called Armadale in West Lothian. It was run by the Glasgow Students Evangelistic Union. Students from various universities would give their time during vacations for evangelistic campaigns. At Armadale, it was decided to hold a special meeting for men only in the Town Hall. Who could they get to speak?

Eric's brother, Rob, had worked in these campaigns. D.P. thought: 'What about his younger brother? Was he a committed Christian? His father was a missionary and his brother was an evangelical Christian. Perhaps he might come to speak that evening? He would be a draw for a men's meeting.'

D.P. went through to Edinburgh with an invitation, making his way to 56 George Square, where Rob and Eric lived. He saw Rob first.

'Do you think Eric would come to speak at our meeting in Armadale?' D.P. asked Rob.

'You'll have to ask him for yourself. He's never done anything like that before,' came the reply.

A few minutes later Eric was standing in front of D.P., and after formal introductions D.P. asked him directly if he would come and address a meeting in Armadale.

Eric stood silently, dropping his head to consider his answer.

'All right, I'll come.'

D.P. believed that Eric had at that time a strong and simple faith in Christ as his Lord, but that he had been a bit of a 'secret disciple.' This was a turning point of commitment to the Lord and evangelism.

In point of fact, Eric felt the same way. All sorts of things went through his mind as to whether he could do it, and do it well. The Lord seemed to confirm his decision the following morning, when he received a letter from his sister, Jenny. The letter contained a Bible verse from Isaiah which read:

'Fear not, for I am with thee; be not dismayed, for I am thy God: I will strengthen thee; yea, I will uphold thee with the right hand of my righteousness' (41:10).

The text confirmed to him his decision. It was in a real sense life-changing, and there would be no turning back.

So, on Friday, 6th April at Armadale, Eric gave his first address at an evangelistic meeting.

D. P. Thomson wrote in his diary:

Eric did remarkably well for a first appearance, and said some telling things.

Though never a great public speaker, it would always be true that Eric had an engaging way of sharing the gospel of Christ. At any rate, the papers were full of the fact that the young track and rugby star was speaking of his Christian faith at religious meetings. Needless to say, wherever he was billed to speak there were well-attended meetings.

That same spring of 1923, D.P. and Eric addressed a meeting at Rutherglen, near Glasgow, attended by around 600 young people. In the May of that year, Eric wrote to D.P. to say that he was a changed man since the day he had asked him to speak at Armadale. He testified that a new joy had come into his life.

But what about his sporting interests? Would his new-found commitment to evangelism interfere with his success on the sports field? No! In both the Edinburgh University Sports and the Scottish University Sports in early season, he won all three sprints: 100 yards, 220 yards and 440 yards. His form was especially impressive in the Scottish Inter-University meeting held at his home track in Edinburgh. He created records in all three events, improving his Scottish 220 yards record to 21.6 on the straight Craiglockhart track, and clocking a very promising 50.2 in only his third senior quarter mile.

The following week, he retained his Scottish 100 and 220 titles at Celtic Park in Glasgow. Yes, he was in the form of his life, and the question arose as to whether or not he might be sent to the highly regarded English Championships.

The opinion was, 'He's good, but it's not worth the £5 cost of sending him.'

So they didn't support him that year. Nevertheless, Eric and his trainer decided to take the trip. After all, these Championships were effectively an 'international' championship meeting. They were to be held at the Chelsea Football Club stadium at Stamford Bridge, London, on Friday 6th, and Saturday 7th July. This would show just how good a sprinter he was.

As it turned out, his performances in the 100 and 220 at Stamford Bridge were sensational. The events on the Saturday went like a dream. He won them all, four races in just a few minutes over an hour and a half:

2.30	100 yards 1st Round (10.0 sec.)
3.10	100 yards 2nd Round (9.8)
3.40	100 yards Final (9.7)
4.05	220 yards Final (21.6)

These were world-class performances. The 100 yards was a British Record, not improved for thirty-four years, and just one-tenth behind the world record.

Perhaps even more significant, was Eric's marvellous running at the annual Triangular International held that year at Stoke on Trent. This was an

International among teams from England (including Wales), Ireland and Scotland. At that time the contest was won according to a points system, 2 points for the winner of an event and 1 point for a runner-up. In the previous four such contests, England had won three and Scotland, with Eric's help in 1921, one. On the points system, it would be rare for anyone to beat England. The year 1923 was an exception, largely through Eric's great performances. He won all three sprints that day, the 440 in remarkable circumstances.

In the 1981 award-winning movie *Chariots of Fire,* there's a great scene in an athletics international between Scotland and France. Included is a 440 yards race in which, early in the race, Eric is knocked over into the in-field area. There is a pause whilst he picks himself up and begins to chase after the other athletes. Though, obviously, becoming distressed with the effort, he manages to catch the others and pass them before the tape.

The whole scene is heroic and very true to the event at Stoke in 1923. That's just how it happened. The real event, though, was the Triangular International. There were two athletes from England (& Wales), Ireland and Scotland, and the track was that day in Stoke hard-baked cinders, not grass as in the film. Otherwise, the unfolding of the race was much as it was depicted in the movie.

The English athlete who knocked Eric over – unintentionally – was J. J. Gillis. He was a fine runner who could run the 440 yards in 50 seconds. In the Stoke race, in which Gillis was disqualified, Eric's winning time on a slow track was 51.2 seconds. But he had caught up twenty yards or so. So, to the keen track running follower, it was clear that Eric was then capable of around 49 seconds for the quarter mile, a performance nearing world-class time for those days. But the supreme effort in the race caused him to collapse afterwards.

One teammate helped him to the pavilion:

'Give him some brandy, that'll revive him,' he suggested.

To this, Eric falteringly whispered: 'No thanks, Jimmy, just a drop of strong tea!'

At any rate, Eric's three victories secured a rare win for Scotland in the International, 12½ points to England's 12, with Ireland on 8½.

Eric took a lot out of himself with his heroic victories at Stoke. But it was clear that he would be strongly in the running for the Olympic Games set for Paris the following year. However, in the autumn something became clear, which would have a serious bearing on the events in which he would finally compete in the Games.

A Question of Conscience

'Eric, it looks like you'll be in the British team for the sprints at the Olympics next year,' said one athletics friend. He went on: 'But do you know that some of the events will be run on Sundays, including the 100 metres heats?'

'Well, I, for one, won't be running in any Sunday competitions,' replied Eric.

The programme for the 1924 Games of the 8th Olympiad to be held in Paris, was available in 1921.

In the autumn of 1923, when publicity started to be given to the Games, the scheduling of events became known. As Eric was clearly a prospect for the short sprints and one or both of the relay events, the scheduling of these events was of some interest to him. What became clear was the heats of the 100 metres and heats and/or finals of the 400 metres and 4 x 400 metres relays, were due to be run off on Sundays during the Games.

Note: All Eric's races in the UK would have been in the old Imperial measurements. The Olympic Games events were in metric distances. Here are the imperial measurements and their metric equivalents: 100 yards = 91.44 metres; 220 yards = 201.17 metres; 440 yards = 402.34 metres.

This presented a clear question of conscience for the young track star. Sunday was the Lord's Day. It was the Christian Sabbath, a day for worship and rest and not work and organised recreations. Eric had been brought up to respect and reverence *The Ten Commandments*, and not least the fourth that required keeping holy one whole day in seven. Eric's settled conviction was that the first day of the week – Sunday – was the Christian Sabbath. The Sabbath principle remained, though the day was changed.

It was understood that the day was changed on account of the resurrection of the Lord Jesus Christ from the dead, on the first day of the week. It stood to reason that, without denying the continuing moral and spiritual requirements of the fourth commandment, Christians would worship on the day of resurrection of the Lord – the first day of the week.

This was Eric's conviction, and therefore he would not be available for any events scheduled for the Lord's Day, Sunday. For him it was not a hard decision to make.

When this became widely known, it came as a bolt from the blue. True, there had always been Christians who had consciences that forbade their taking part in such things as sports on Sundays. However, it was not often that a British runner was fancied for sprinting events at such a great event as the Olympics. Some people were critical of Eric's position:

'He's letting the side down,' said some.

Others thought: 'Surely you could make an exception here.' Yet others felt: 'The continental Sabbath finishes at midday; surely that will suffice for your conscience.' None of this swayed Eric. He would stick to his principles, whatever the cost. His Sabbath lasted all day! He was more concerned about the Lord's view of him, than what other people thought. The Lord and His Word must be first. He also felt that training or competing in sports on Sundays would set a bad example for other young people. He felt his credibility as a Christian was at stake. He did not want such things upon his conscience.

This whole episode, however, raised two problems.

It raised a problem for the British Olympic Association. The thought of losing Eric for the 100 metres, the 'blue ribbon' event of the track events, and both the relays, did not appeal to them. They approached the International Olympic Committee towards the end of the year to ask if religious conscientious objectors to Sunday events might have their races or events re-scheduled for another day. In January 1924, the reply came back:

> *The re-scheduling of events to accommodate an athlete who for conscientious reasons will not compete on a Sunday, is not acceptable to the French authorities.*

The issue also raised a problem for Eric himself, not about whether or not he would run in Sunday events, for there was no question in his mind about that; but whether he would seriously take on another event like the 400 metres which was free of any Sunday scheduling. After his race at Stoke, the question did arise as to whether he could do well over the longer sprint.

At that time, though, the 400 metres was not considered a 'sprint' at all, but was more akin to the half mile. It wasn't so common for an all-out sprinter to go for the 400 metres. It was considered one of the hardest events in the range of track and field distances, a 'killer sprint'. In those days even the top quarter milers tended to pace themselves over the distance rather than go out hard from the off. Eric talked it over with Tom McKerchar and others who might give him good advice, and he made his decision. He would try the quarter mile in 1924.

As he was coming up to the fourth and final year of his BSc course at Edinburgh, he therefore decided to forego rugby for the 1923–24 season, much to the disappointment of the Scottish Rugby Union. He considered that he would be well occupied training for the 400 metres over the winter months. It might help keep his mind off rugby, which he loved, and could not bear to watch when he was not playing!

Eric needed Tom to help him 'run the distance' over 400 metres. After all, by the end of the 1923 season he had only competed in the event as a senior four times, with a modest best of 50.2! Not much of a prospect for the Games at that rate! In addition to this, in the Games he would have 'back-to-back' races – two each on successive days. If he was to reach the final of the 400 metres he would have to up his standard. It would be a hard ask for such an inexperienced runner at the distance. However, he would give it his best shot.

Eric was always wholehearted in what he did, whether in student evangelism, studies or sport. He was a good role model for young people for dedication and determination in the tasks he undertook. He was, of course, concerned that God would be honoured by what he did and said. Among other things he applied himself to training, but that wasn't the only thing on his mind.

His primary concern now was not sport, but working out his Christian faith. By 1924, Eric felt himself being called to serve God in China, the land of his birth. He felt a burden for the Chinese people and for taking the gospel to them. He applied to the London Missionary Society in March 1924. His application had asked what his reasons were for seeking such work. His answers were interesting:

1. *My father worked abroad and that very fact gave an impetus to my desires in that direction.*
2. *My qualifications in sport give me a natural link with boys at school and college. This gave me an opportunity of using these talents for leading men to the feet of the Master.*
3. *Being trained as a teacher, I felt that a larger scope was offered for definite Christian work in a College*

> *founded on the Word of God, than in a school which was not based on such a foundation.*
>
> 4. *The call of China was so great — China is passing through a critical time, a formative period, which might decide as much for the future of the country, that the very greatness of the work appealed.*

His original intention was to take up a position in the Anglo-Chinese College at Tientsin in North China. This was a Christian-ethos college for boys between eight and eighteen. He would teach Science and Games.

Eric's initial intention was to go out immediately after graduation, later in 1924. D. P. Thomson, however, persuaded him otherwise:

'Look, Eric, you'd be well advised to stay in Scotland for another year. We could arrange some evangelistic campaigns and you could do some divinity training. That would give you invaluable experience for China.'

'I'm sure that's right. I need some preparation,' replied Eric.

Arrangements therefore begun to be set in place for D.P. and Eric, with others, to embark on a year's campaigning for the Lord after Eric's graduation — and of course after the Games in Paris.

Olympic Games Beckon

'You are invited to accompany the combined Oxford and Cambridge University teams for a trip to Philadelphia for the annual Relay meeting of the University of Pennsylvania in April 1924. Special sprinting events have been arranged, in which you are invited to compete.'

So ran the invitation to Eric for the Penn Relays in the Spring of 1924.

Unfortunately, the journey over on the *SS Berengaria* was a pretty choppy one and poor Eric was violently sick and a bit weakened by the experience. Nevertheless, he did run in Invitation 100 yards and 220 yards races.

It was all a great experience for him, not only in terms of the athletics, but he also saw something of the 'new world'. It was the time of 'prohibition' of alcohol in the USA and as a teetotaller he thought, on the whole, that prohibition was a good thing!

When they passed into the University of Pennsylvania in Philadelphia, Eric saw emblazoned over the gate the famous words of William Penn: 'In the dust of defeat, as well as in the laurels of victory, there is a glory to be found if one has done his best.'

The athletes stayed at the comfortable Pennsylvanian Cricket Club facilities.

Eric did his best in the meet. After all, it was his first competition of the year. He was placed fourth in the 100 yards, in a very close-run race, and he was a good second in the 220 yards. Not bad, considering he had little opportunity to train during the journey, and considering how sick he had been on the way over!

It was a great experience, though, giving him some insight into the sort of athletes he would run against, Lord-willing, should he make the Olympics in Paris. The return journey was on a vessel named the *SS Republic*. Unfortunately, on the return trip he lost two cases containing all his souvenirs of his Philadelphia trip!

As far as athletics back home were concerned, Eric had few competitions in Scotland from the beginning of the 1924 season, up to the start of the Games, which were scheduled to start early in July. In just over two weeks from the end of May to the beginning of June, he won the three sprints (100 yards, 220 yards and 440 yards) successively in the Edinburgh University Sports, the Scottish Inter-University Sports and the Scottish Championships. None of the performances were anything to write home about. There was no indication in his form in Scotland that he would be a leading contender for any Olympic crown.

The first real test was the English Championships on 20th and 21st June at Stamford Bridge. Though he entered all three events, he withdrew from the 100 because there were so many other races to tackle in 220 and 440. On the Friday night he had four races, the first two rounds of both the 220 yards and 440 yards. This was the first time he had ever run two 440s in the same evening. He won all his races within three-and-a-half hours – a wonderful performance. His times weren't anything special, though the cinder track wasn't particularly fast.

The finals were on the next day. Surprisingly, Eric was defeated in the 220 by a South African, Howard Kinsman. He did, however, win the 440 easily. Still, his winning time in the quarter was only a modest 49.6 seconds. There was no indication in these performances that he would be a contender for either the 200 metres or 400 metres at Paris, and the Games were just a fortnight away.

Meantime, everything was very tight. He had his finals at Edinburgh University to think about. Though he had always done well in his class work, serious preparations for the track had affected his results just a bit. Still, his figures never fell below 68 per cent and, despite the distractions of extra preparations for the Games in Paris, he was set fair to graduate on 17th July, six days after the final of the 400 metres.

As a Christian, Eric sought to live for Jesus as his Lord and to honour Him in his university and church concerns, as well as in his athletics. He was always careful to lay these things before the Lord in prayer.

What could he do, but go forward seeking to do his best, trusting in the Lord Jesus Christ? He never prayed that he would win the Olympic events, or any other event for that matter. He recognised that would be simply selfish and unworthy. He did pray, however, that in the meetings, as in all else in his life, the Lord would be glorified, and that He might be pleased to use Eric's witness for his Lord to the blessing of others.

It only remained for him to make his way to London to meet up with the other British Olympic competitors, for the onward journey to Paris. They received a great send-off from Victoria Station in London, as they set off hopefully a few days before the Opening Ceremony, due in the Colombes athletics stadium on Saturday, 5th July.

'He ran like a man Inspired'

Bang! The report of the pistol. The 400 metres final was under way.

All eyes suddenly turned on the runners as they lurched forward from their 'set' position and started to pound their way down the cinder track.

Because this 400 metres was run round one bend, Eric just decided to run it like an extended 200 metres. Tom McKerchar had warned him not to go off too fast.

'Eric, you have to pace yourself. Don't go off too fast. Hold something back in reserve for the finish.'

According to prevailing track wisdom, people just didn't sprint the first half of the race. What was Eric Liddell, the flying Scotsman, doing? He was running along in the outside lane at what looked like full tilt. Was this not sprinting suicide?

Harold Abrahams thought so. Harold, an Englishman, had won the 100 metres on the Monday in Eric's absence. He had bought a special seat in the stand opposite the finishing line. He saw Eric career off at top speed. 'Slow down, Eric, you'll never keep that up!' he thought to himself – and said it to the colleagues around him. Harold thought Eric a fine man, a man of Christian principle, quiet, unassuming, but a world-class runner. He wanted to see him do well. He also wanted to see his fellow compatriot, Guy Butler – who was in the second lane – do well. But Eric was out in front in that outside lane. Could he keep that pace up? Harold seriously doubted that he could.

The race was nothing if not exciting. The impartial French, with no home athlete to cheer on, didn't much mind who they cheered for. The British and American spectators just wanted their own men to come out on top. But there was this smallish Scot with the unusual style – head back and arms all over the place – cutting out the pace. The American on his immediate inside, Horatio Fitch, was the only one to get near Eric as the athletes came off the crown of the bend into the straight. He thought, 'Who is this Eric Liddell? He's gone off so fast he's bound to come back towards the end of the race.' To Fitch's dismay, Eric didn't falter.

Eric couldn't see the other runners, but he heard the American's spikes rhythmically hitting the track right behind him on his left. It spurred him on. He pushed himself, and, keeping his form as well as he could, the others were left well and truly struggling in his wake. The world record had been beaten by the Swiss, Joseph Imbach, on the previous day (48.0), and by Fitch in the first semi-final less than three hours earlier (47.8). It had looked as though the listed World and Olympic records were bound to go in the final.

Back in Edinburgh, some of Eric's student friends were crowded round a crackly self-made radio receiver trying to pick up a live commentary on the 400 metres final. Their excitement rose to fever-pitch as the announcer commentated on the end of the race. 'They've cleared the last curve. Liddell is still leading! He's increasing his lead! Increasing and increasing! Oh, what a race!'

The cheer among these students matched the cheers in the Olympic Stadium as Eric on the outside lane, head thrown back and arms and legs pumping, went though the tape yards ahead of the next man.

Harold Abrahams, was thrilled. To him, Eric had run like a man inspired. There was an element of truth in that.

Eric could hardly believe it. He couldn't forget that Scripture verse in the note the physio had handed him: 'He that honours me, I will honour.' He sent up a prayer of thanks to the Lord for enabling him to finish the race well. He congratulated the other athletes, shaking them heartily by the hand. Hands on hips, he posed for a photo or two. Then he went back to the changing area and thought to himself:

'Wow! What a thing: Olympic champion.'

A few moments later, Eric heard over the public address system the announcement:

'400 metres result. First place and a new Olympic Games record and World record time; Eric Liddell, Great Britain, 47.6 seconds …'

Eric shook his head. Did he really do that? It would take some time to sink in. In fact, he felt a little embarrassed that he was the centre of such attention. But he would now have to give some thoughts to an address he was to give the following Sunday, at the Scots Kirk in Paris. In a way, that was as important to him, if not more so, than any success on the running track.

It was an unexpected triumph for the modest Scot. One reporter wrote of Eric's success – with just a touch of exaggeration –'… probably the most dramatic race ever seen on a running track'!

Eric, with characteristic modesty, would take that with a pinch of salt!

Years later, someone asked Eric what the secret of his success was at the distance. He said, famously:'What is the secret of my success in running the 400 metres? I run the first half of the race as fast as I can, and then, with God's help, I run the second half harder!'

Whatever other races this might have applied to, it was exactly how Eric ran the 400 metres final at Paris in 1924.

The Games finished the following Sunday (13th July), though, as on the first Sunday, Eric was on other business than sport. He was in the Scots Kirk at rue Bayard, taking part in a service in which he gave an address. That Sunday, the Great Britain teams in the 4 x 100 metres and 4 x 400 metre relays won, respectively, silver and bronze medals. This left a nagging question for some: 'What might have happened if Eric had been running?'

This was a speculative question. It was one, however, which was answered the following Saturday (19th July) when in a relay meeting at Stamford Bridge in London, teams representing the British Empire and the USA would cross swords. This time, Eric would be in the relay races. Purposely, it may be assumed, the British Empire 4 x 440 yards relay team for that contest would comprise four Brits, three of the athletes who won bronze at the Games for Great Britain, plus Eric. An interesting prospect was in store.

However, there was the slight matter of a return to Scotland and to Graduation for Eric before then ...

Acclaim and Graduation

There was no more popular an athlete, in the 1920s in Scotland, than Eric Liddell. Even his contemporaries, like Harold Abrahams, recognised how important his Christianity was for both his life in general and his sport in particular. He was widely seen as a 'muscular Christian'. People soon recognised that he was a faithful follower of his Master, Jesus Christ. Biblical faith directed his life, most notably after that change in his life in the Spring of 1923.

The first gauntlet to run was at his graduation as a Bachelor of Science, held at the McEwan Hall in Edinburgh on Thursday, 17th July. It was obvious his 'capping' wasn't going to pass unnoticed. Beforehand, it was arranged that he be presented with the equivalent of a laurel wreath, actually made of the wild olive *oleaster* donated by the Royal Botanical Garden in the city. This was to be placed on his head as he graduated, and he was to be presented with an 'ode' in Greek especially composed by Professor Mair in honour of his achievement at Paris. The Principal of the University was Sir Alfred Ewing.

When Eric stood forward to be 'capped', pandemonium broke out from the unusually large crowd in the Hall. Sir Alfred tried to make himself heard above the noise:

'Mr Liddell, you have shown that none can pass you, but the examiners!'

In those days after the Graduation ceremony, a service was held in St Giles Cathedral on the Royal Mile. To this, Eric was carried shoulder high by fellow students. Before going into the service, he was called on to give a speech. Eric obliged, with typical modesty:

'When I was in America earlier this year I saw written over the entrance of the University of Pennsylvania: 'In the dust of defeat as well as in the laurels of victory there is a glory to be found if one has done their best.' There are many here who have done their best, though they haven't succeeded in gaining the laurels of victory. To all such, there is as much honour due as to those who have received the laurels of victory.'

His ordeal wasn't over yet, however. The following day a 'Complimentary Dinner' was held in Mackie's Dining Saloon on Princes Street, Edinburgh. It seemed that everybody who was anybody in Edinburgh society, was there. It was all very intimidating for a young man of very humble background!

Lord Sands was the Chairman. Also present was the Lord Provost, Sir William Sleigh, the Principal of the University, Sir Alfred Ewing, and numerous other Knights of the Realm, clergymen, and other dignitaries. The purpose of the meeting was stated on the Menu Card:

> *In admiration of his remarkable athletic achievements, and to his devotion to principle in that connection as a reverent upholder of the Christian Sabbath.*

It was quite a thing for Lord Sands to say in his opening remarks of appreciation, an admiration for Eric's stand for the Lord's Day:

'In these days of moral flabbiness, it is something to find a man who is not content to shield himself behind such easy phrases as, "It is only once in the way," or, "When you go to Rome you must do as they do in Rome."'

The Rev Dr Norman Maclean in his remarks suggested that,

'His achievement has proved that Christians are not milk-sops, that they are not prigs, and that Christianity is something which has to do with all departments of life.'

In his reply to the various speeches, Eric simply referred to the note given by the physio before he ran on the day of the 400 metre final as one of the finest things he enjoyed at the Olympic Games. He said how glad he was that there were others who held the same sentiments as himself on the matter of the Lord's Day.

It was decided at the meeting to send a cable to Eric's parents in China which read:

Large gathering, Edinburgh, Chairman Lord Sands, cordially congratulates father and mother on Eric's wonderful feat, and still more on his noble witness for Christian principles.

Immediately after the dinner, Eric made his way to Waverley Station to take the train to London for the relay contest between the British Empire and the U.S.A., scheduled for the following day.

Such was the rarity of success by Scottish sportsmen in Olympic Games, that Eric's victory in Paris was bound to cause praise among the press and public. He was a hugely popular individual, even though he held some unpopular views such as strong Sabbath observance and strict temperance. However, Eric had an attractive personality, a winsome manner, and he was clearly a young man of principle. People respected this.

Though Eric was now a prominent personality in Scotland, his fellow students noticed that it didn't turn his head. Later on in the year, there was a tribute in the Edinburgh University paper, *The Student*. The issue in question was dated 22nd October 1924.

A fellow student came up to Eric one day and said: 'Eric, have you seen the latest *Student*?'

Taking the issue in his hands, Eric read, somewhat embarrassed:

Success in athletics sufficient to turn the head of an ordinary man has left Liddell absolutely unspoilt, and his modesty is entirely genuine and unaffected. He has taken his triumph in his stride, as it were, and never made any sort of fuss. What he has thought it right to do, that he has done, looking neither to the left nor to the right, and yielding not one jot or tittle of principle either to court applause or to placate criticism. Courteous and affable, he is utterly free from 'gush.' Devoted to his principles, he is without a touch of Pharisaism. The best that can be said of any student is that he has left the fame of his University fairer than he found it, and his grateful Alma mater is proud to recognise that to no man does that praise more certainly belong than to Eric Henry Liddell.

Eric found this frankly all a bit humbling and embarrassing, though he tried to enjoy every minute of it too.

More Great Running

There was a great buzz at Stamford Bridge on the Saturday for the Relay meeting between teams representing the British Empire and the U.S.A.

It was quite a thrill for the huge crowd to see so many Olympic athletes and champions in action. There were numerous relay races and other field events and it all provided a thrilling afternoon for competitors and spectators alike.

In an afternoon really dominated by the American athletes, the 4 x 440 yards relay was awaited with particular interest. The Empire team comprised four Britons, including Edward Toms on the first leg, Richard Ripley on the second, Guy Butler on the third and Eric on the anchor leg. The Americans had a strong team with three of their individual competitors in the 400 metres in the Games – Eric Wilson, Ray Robertson and Horatio Fitch – together with Bill Stevenson, a Rhodes scholar at Oxford, who had brought their 4 x 400 metre team home for the gold medal at the Paris Games. This time Fitch would be on the last leg against Eric.

As it happened, the race came down to a final lap duel between the gold and silver medallists from

Paris. This time Fitch took over from Stevenson with a healthy lead of about six yards. It seemed an impossible ask for Eric. But he set off purposefully in pursuit. With a good burst of speed he caught up some ground down the back straight. Fitch kept ahead round the bend, but he couldn't hold off the Scot down the home straight and after a wonderful leg, Eric came home by about four yards. It was one of only two victories in eight events for the British Empire that afternoon. But it so nearly produced a world record. The Empire team's 3 minute 18.2 seconds was just one-fifth of a second behind the listed world record. As for Eric's performance, it established him as the top quarter miler in the world. The time for his leg was taken as 48.4, though it was reckoned that the split time was taken from around seven yards before the 440 line. It was probably the fastest 440 yards ever run up to that point.

Horatio Fitch congratulated the Flying Scot:

'Well done, Eric, what a wonderful race you ran. Beat me fair and square.'

Eric certainly had given the largely British crowd something to cheer about. But the Americans also couldn't help admiring him.

The following Friday (25th July) Eric had another reception to honour his achievements. This time it was given by the Lord Provost and Town Council of Edinburgh in the City Chambers. It involved a gathering of all sorts of celebrities and dignitaries, representing, it was said, 'intellectual and physical culture and other interests of the city'.

There were Lords, Ladies, Knights, clergy, and Professors, it was all very formal and imposing. Eric was presented with a gold watch and chain. In his reply to the speeches, Eric made strong emphasis on his indebtedness to his trainer, Tom McKerchar, to whom he owed so much.

Eric had a few more competitions before the end of the season. One of these was in Greenock at which a Scotland verses Canada competition had been arranged. The track was a grass one and the rain poured down, but still the crowd saw their hero win the 440 yards and bring the Scottish team home first in the 1 mile medley relay. It was quite common for special evangelistic meetings to be arranged in connection with sports meetings. This happened after that Greenock meeting.

On the Sunday following, Eric addressed a crowd at Inverkip Road. Though heavy rain fell throughout, several thousand turned up so that an adjournment was necessary to an adjacent park. On that occasion, Eric spoke from Ecclesiastes 12:1 'Remember now thy creator in the days of thy youth.'

Though he had a few more competitions before the end of the season, which inevitably attracted huge crowds, his mind turned to other things. He was committed to a year's study at the Congregational College at Hope Terrace in Edinburgh, and with

D. P. Thomson embarking on a year of evangelistic campaigns in Scotland and beyond. He would not play rugby that winter, but he did intend one more season, or part season, on the track before departing for the mission field in China the following July, if the Lord willed.

A Year's Campaigning

'Just speak from your heart,' counselled D.P., 'and use your own experiences to illustrate the Christian message.'

Eric had been getting used to addressing meetings ever since he had been first invited to address a meeting by D. P. Thomson. D.P. was a great help. He was a divinity student with a real zeal for evangelism. He was a different sort of character, more outgoing than Eric, who, by his own admission was a bit backward in coming forward, a bit on the shy side. But some of the boldness of his energetic colleague, with the encouragement of his keen and committed brother, Rob, and memories of his own father's preaching, encouraged Eric for his own speaking engagements.

Eric became well known, not for being a particularly good speaker, but as a quiet, effective young man to whom young hearers could relate. Eric recognised that his messages needed to be simple. That turned out to be their strength. They were usually well-illustrated from experiences in the classroom and his early days, as well as the sports field. It was very effective.

Eric was quiet and unassuming, and had a real love of people. All of that was infectious. Still, the thought of public speaking always made him feel nervous – more nervous than running or rugby! However, from the outset, his concern was to commit such things to the Lord, and seek strength from Him for anything he said or did. It was a matter of witness.

Eric did feel his inadequacies in theological training, despite some great help from D.P. He therefore attended the Scottish Congregational College in the leafy Grange area of Edinburgh, to help him prepare for his mission service. He began a year's course there in the autumn of 1924. At the same time he and D.P. made preparations with much prayer for a year's evangelistic meetings in Scotland and England.

In the autumn of 1924, Eric shared in the Students' Campaigns organised with D.P. The last and biggest of these was held in Kilmarnock, Ayrshire, in early October. On the opening Sunday, Eric faced a crowd of 500 people. But there were six meetings every day. The crowd on the second Sunday evening amounted to some 1,700 people, young and old. What an experience for Eric, to be engaged in such meetings and have the responsibility to share the message of the gospel of Jesus Christ. Certainly many people were drawn by the mere fact that the Olympic champion was going to speak. But they knew it wasn't a public relations exercise, but a serious call to come to faith in the Lord Jesus Christ.

At the end of the various meetings that October, D.P. wrote home to his mother:

Eric has made great strides as a chairman, a leader, and a speaker. You would hardly know he was the same man as six months ago. We are getting on very, very happily together. I have never known a finer character in all my varied experience. There has never been a hitch or a shadow in our friendship, and it is due to him almost entirely. He is pure gold through and through.

This is how things went on throughout the year. They went from church to church and school to school, and held meetings in YMCAs, theatres and public halls of all kinds. In well-attended meetings, many lives were touched and changed. D.P. wrote later:

Young men and boys in particular were led in large numbers of cases, I am persuaded, than either of us was ever likely to know of, to invest their lives in the service of the Lord and Master, Eric set forth so winsomely.

Meetings were regularly held into 1925 and right up to the very eve of his departure for China. Not that Eric only ever spoke at meetings organised with Thomson. He had other great passions in his Christian life and became involved in the active support of them.

One, of course, was to encourage Bible reading and prayer. In January 1925, in a church in Edinburgh, he addressed the Fellowship of Bible Reading and Prayer. To Eric the Bible was God's Word and prayer was speaking to the Father in Heaven. He saw these as vital parts of healthy Christian faith and life.

He was also concerned about the Lord's Day. He was known as 'the man who wouldn't run on Sunday'. He addressed meetings of the Lord's Day Association of Scotland in support of the Lord's Day as a day of rest from work and sport. He had been taught that the first day of the week was the Christian Sabbath; that Christians observed the first day of the week in commemoration of the rising of Jesus from the dead and on the basis of the fourth commandment. At a meeting on Monday, 18th May (1925) at the time of the General Assembly meetings of the Presbyterian Churches, he spoke at a Lord's Day rally and said among other things:

'Our difficulty today was that inside the church there are those who think very little of it.'

'If the churches were really united on the issue the attitudes to the Christian Sabbath would surely be better,' he added, pointedly.

Another thing that really concerned him was the widespread use of alcohol. Eric was all his life a non-smoker and teetotaller. He often addressed meetings organised to discourage the use of alcohol. It was something he considered to be a curse in society. The issue had traditionally been a concern in his family. For several generations the Liddells had been active 'temperance' people.

The last campaign Eric was involved in, with D.P., was held in Edinburgh a few weeks before he left for China. It was well publicised with a 'flier' that had a picture of Eric in running garb. The series of twelve successive evening meetings started on a Tuesday in early May (1925) in the famous St George's United Free Church in the west end of the city. At D.P.'s suggestion, the organising committee hired the huge Usher Hall in Lothian Road for the Sunday evening Rallies, advertised to start at 8 o'clock. This hall, the main Concert Hall in the capital city, was a few hundred yards away from St George's.

On the Monday evening in the second week, there was a capacity audience of 1,100. Numbers tailed off a bit in the course of the week and by the Friday they were down to 500 or so. How would they fill the Usher Hall on the Sunday? The minister of St George's generously promised to end his evening service sharply and come up at the head of his congregation to the Usher Hall to swell the crowds at that last rally. In point of fact, there was a huge attendance that night. Both the Usher Hall and a church immediately across the road were filled. It was amazing. Surely the Lord's hand was in this, they believed, and that there would be real Christian fruit as a result of the thirteen days work.

A report of one of these meetings gave an account of an address by Eric. It was said that, 'Mr Liddell, quiet and restrained, *spoke* slowly and sometimes in scarcely more than a whisper, although always distinctly audible.' The same paper reported him as saying:

> *Young, inexperienced, and without eloquence, we have come before you because we feel that we have a message*

for you … We feel youth has an appeal to youth, and we want to give you our experience. We are placing before you during these few days the thing we have found to be best. We are setting before you one who is worthy of all our devotion, Christ. He is the Saviour for the young as well as the old, and He is the one who can bring out what is best in us … Are you living up to the standards of Jesus Christ? We are looking for men and women who are willing to answer the challenge Christ is sending out … Have you sought a leader in everyday life? In Jesus Christ you will find a leader worthy of your devotion and mine. I looked for one I could admire, and I found Christ. I am a debtor, and no wonder I am a debtor, for He has given me a message which can only be experienced. If this audience was out-and-out for Christ, the whole of Edinburgh would be changed. If the whole of this audience was out for Christ, it would go far past Edinburgh and through all Scotland. The last time Edinburgh was swept, all Scotland was flooded. What are you going to do tonight?

This well expresses Eric's passion for the gospel and Person of the Lord Jesus Christ, and of his concern for souls.

However, this was the last the country was to hear from the Olympic missionary for another seven years. A few short weeks later, after he had swept all before him at his last Scottish Championships in Glasgow, he set off for his life's work for the Lord in China.

'For China Now'

For China now another race he runs,
As sure and straight as those Olympic ones,
And if the ending's not so simply known —
We'll judge he'll make it, since his speeds his own.

This verse appeared in a popular Glasgow newspaper just before Eric left for the mission field. There was also a cartoon of him dressed as a minister (which he was not, then) and pounding round an athletics track. It goes without saying that Eric knew that the ending was in his Master's hands.

Though Eric would set out for China from Victoria Station, London, on Saturday, 4th July, his journey would actually start from Edinburgh on Monday, 29th June. Before then there were numerous farewell meetings, and of course his very last track meet in Scotland, the Scottish Championships at Hampden Park, Glasgow, on the Saturday. At these championships there was a huge crowd, attracted by the fact that it was his last meeting before going to China. He won every race in a day of 'uninterrupted triumph'. It thrilled the crowds. Just to catch a glimpse of their modest sporting hero, Scotland's greatest athlete.

The following day was a bitter-sweet one for Eric. A special meeting was held at the Augustine Congregational Church on George IV Bridge in Edinburgh. Again, there was a full church of well-wishers, with an overflow meeting at Martyrs and St John's United Free Church across the road. Eric spoke on the theme of dedication to Christ and His service.

Eric was always embarrassed on such occasions when so many flattering things were said. This time was no different. Afterwards, everybody wanted to meet him, wish him well and shake his hand. It was moving, encouraging and comforting to have such prayers and good wishes for his forthcoming missionary service. Eric was moved to tears.

His departure began the following day from the College at Hope Terrace. Students and other friends made sure it would be a great send-off. They arranged a carriage for him which would be drawn by the students themselves from the College down to Waverley Station from where he was due to pick up an east coast train. The carriage was decorated. Eric, already prematurely balding, but wearing a suit and trilby hat, allowed himself to be pulled down to the Station. It was a great send-off. There were people who had heard of this 'procession' lining the route and there was a considerable crowd at the station.

It was an amazing send-off for a great athlete whom the Scottish public had taken to their hearts. He was effectively turning his back on a glittering career and perhaps more sporting honours. But what were these to him? He was seeking the Lord's will for his life, and sincerely felt it to be in mission work in China.

The crowd cheered. They sang, 'For he's a jolly good fellow!'

Eric was compelled to give a few words as he left:

'I'm going out as an ambassador to another country. Our motto should be, "Christ for the world, for the world needs Christ." I hope that I can be an example of this to the end of my days.'

By God's grace he did. Eric leaned out the window and led them in two verses of a favourite hymn:

> *Jesus shall reign where'er the sun*
> *doth her successive journey's run;*
> *His kingdom stretch from shore to shore,*
> *till moons shall wax and wane no more.*

> *For Him shall endless prayer be made,*
> *And praises throng to crown His head;*
> *His name, like sweet perfume, shall rise*
> *With every morning sacrifice.*

Slowly but surely, the train pulled away and he was soon out of their sight. Now he was bound for China and his life's work for His Lord. And he looked forward with anticipation to meeting up with his parents, sister, Jenny, younger brother, Ernest, and Rob who was now married and working with the London Missionary Society in Shanghai as a medical missionary.

An Adventurous Journey

Eric's journey to China was nothing if not adventurous.

Taking the east coast route from Waverley, Eric travelled to Berwick-upon-Tweed where he spent a night with his mother's relatives before taking the overnight sleeper to London. Eric left for his long journey from Victoria Station in London on Saturday, 4th July. This took him to Folkestone where he picked up the ferry to Flushing in the Netherlands. From there his railway journey would take him to Berlin, where he would spend a 'long day' of ten hours. Then it was a train to Riga in Latvia and from Riga to Moscow where he would pick up the Trans-Siberian railway. And that was the beginning of the adventure! That journey would take a week through Russia to China. It was – and remains – the longest railway journey in the world, covering not far short of 6,000 miles in seven days! The alternative was a far longer voyage by ship. There were no aircraft in those days, just arduous, yet romantic, journeys! But what an adventurous start to missionary life it was.

Eric settled into the carriage at Moscow and was at long last on the famous Trans-Siberian railway. He looked forward to a long journey from west to east towards his destination, eventually, in Tientsin.

He had plenty time for reflection and reading and prayer. It was all uncharted territory for him, this trip through Russia to China. As he settled in his seat Eric read again his father's Annual Report written in December 1924. He read:

> *The past year has seen another Civil War, and the change of President, as well as a whole series of changes in the personnel of provincial positions, both civil and military. At the same time the country has been brought to a sad condition with regard to railway communications and commerce ... the feeling all around is one of suspense, not knowing what will happen next. To those who look on, it seems that no one party is strong enough to command obedience, and really govern the country. The government of any one party is flouted by some other, although that other may have sworn loyalty to the one in power. It is not surprising that during part of this year Church work has been so difficult.*

Church work so difficult! What was he going out to? He read on:

> *This year we had the triple evils of war, flood and famine. Any one of these is bad enough, but all three together made for suffering that is very hard to realise. Ruin has overtaken great numbers of families, and it will never be known how many lives have been lost, and may still be lost, through these visitations. Oh, the horror of it all! And to think that so much of it is needless suffering, destruction and waste.*

Yes, it was into this situation that Eric was heading. But it was for the Lord and He would give all needed grace. He was thankful for that reality. Between that report and Eric's journey out, his father had written in a way that indicated things were worse rather than better. Eric looked at his father's more recent letter:

Last year I said there was a 'stirring of the waters.' This year one should say that 'the waters are boiling.' Words fail to convey to one not conversant with ways Chinese the conditions that exist at present, and the variety of influences at work to make a forecast impossible. The grievances of China have been magnified beyond all recognition. So complex is the situation, so varied are the views expressed, so opposite the conclusions reached, so many the solutions suggested, that one staggers beneath the crushing load. A nation is in travail, seeking to produce that which will meet all its aspirations. Whether it will do so or not is another question.

It was to such a situation that Eric was committed: From the plaudits of sporting fame and the stability of the British Empire, to the uncertainties and dangers of 'a nation in travail' was quite a move.

Eric had started his journey on 4th July. Exactly two weeks later he disembarked at Pei-Tai-Ho, on the coast of the Bo Hai Sea where some of the missionary societies had built a few cottages for the convenience of their workers.

'Eric, how wonderful to see you! Praise the Lord you have had a safe journey!' exclaimed his father and mother.

Many family and friends were there to meet him, pleased and relieved to have the weary traveller among them at last.

Six happy weeks were spent there, Rob and his wife, Ria, joining them from Shanghai after a week. Then it was time for Eric and his father to take the five-hour train journey to Tientsin inland to the west. The College to which Eric was appointed would re-open in early September and he had unpacking and preparation to attend to.

New Beginning

'The City of the Heavenly Ford.' That was Tientsin. It was on the Hai He river, thirty miles from the coast.

This was where Eric would live and work for the next twelve years, save for a year's 'home leave' in 1931–32.

Tientsin had a population at the time of one-and-a-half million. It was a great centre of trade and industry as well as Christian missionary work. The missionary community was a large and varied one, among which was work carried on by the London Missionary Society. Eric's parents had been posted here after their home leave of 1922.

At that time Tientsin was divided into two unequal parts. The smaller and more densely populated area was occupied by native Chinese, and the more spacious sector contained the foreign 'Concessions' of which there were eight: Austrian, Italian, Russian, Japanese, French, British, German and Belgian. At first Eric stayed with his parents and sister, Jenny, and younger brother, Ernest, within the 'British' Concession.

The Anglo-Chinese College where Eric began his work in China had been founded by Dr Samuel Lavington Hart under the London Missionary Society and had opened its doors in 1902 with Dr Hart as Principal. He was still there when Eric first entered the college as teacher.

The college was for boys – predominantly Chinese – from between twelve and eighteen. It was modelled on British High or Grammar Schools, which in China were known as 'Middle' Schools. The teaching was in English. The students, of which there were normally around 500 were mostly from the 'upper echelons' of local Chinese society. It was recognised as one of the best educational institutes in North China, taking students up to University level. There was a staff of five British and twenty-five Chinese masters.

The ethos of the college was entirely Christian. The concern of Dr Hart had been to influence generations of Chinese for Christ and Christian principles.

The Christian input into the college life was considerable. There was a *Daily Assembly* for senior and junior boys. This involved prayers, readings from the Scriptures and hymns, and lasted about twenty-five minutes. Then there were the weekly Bible Circles held in each class normally conducted by the tutor. They were voluntary and held out of college hours. Most of the boys did attend, at least around 300. In Eric's experience around 90 per cent of his boys attended his group. Apart from this, there was a Sunday morning service in the college chapel, and a weekly midweek meeting for prayer and worship, though a smaller percentage of boys attended these.

As far as his own responsibilities at College were concerned, in the years Eric taught at T.A.C.C. he took classes in Science and English, but also had responsibility for Physical Education and the sporting side of the college curriculum, as well as the Christian aspects of college life. Eric had such a way with people, not least young people. His influence among them for Christ was profound. Very early in his missionary service he wrote about his Bible class work:

> *I have been taking the Life and Times of Jesus with them. They each have a daily Bible reading card, with instruction as to how to use it with advantage. By this I hope to get them into the habit of (1) Quiet morning prayer; (2) Expectation that the Bible has a message for them which can be applied in their own lives day by day.*

This was the sort of thing that was involved with that part of the work.

Besides this, though the teaching medium was English, he did set himself to learn or re-learn Chinese. As a young boy he had learned some Mandarin from a devoted Chinese amah. The young Liddell boys needed to have some Chinese, simply to communicate with the Chinese children in the mission compound, in which much of their early years were spent.

By the time Eric went into the district church and evangelistic work at the end of 1937, he was really quite proficient in the Mandarin form of Chinese.

Running Missionary

Athletics and sport were never far from Eric's life, even in China. He continued to compete right up to 1930. But quite early in his time at the T.A.C.C. he became involved in helping to design a running track in Tientsin which would be suitable for major track and field events. This was in 1926. He modelled the track on the stadium and track at Stamford Bridge in London, at which he had performed in 1923–4. The Tientsin track was called the Min Yuan Stadium and it is still there, though much altered and now with an 'all-weather' track. It was reckoned at the time to be one of the best tracks in Asia.

In connection with his own running in China, there were several stories involving him that became almost legendary. There was the incident in September 1928, at a meeting in Manchuria, in which athletes from France and Japan, as well as China, were competing shortly after the Olympic Games at Amsterdam. Eric had been invited to take part at Dairen, Manchuria, in the South Manchurian Railway Celebration meeting. It was to celebrate the Coronation of the Emperor of Japan. The meeting featured a contest between Japanese and French Olympic athletes. Eric Liddell ran and won 200 metres and 400 metres invitation events. 'The Japanese and French Olympic Teams were there,' he was to recall, 'with their Olympic laurels, fresh from Amsterdam, and it happened, somehow, that I won the 200 and the 400 metres.'

He gave his own account of one particular incident in this meeting:

My race was just half an hour before my boat. I tried to have the boat held, but failed. It was 20 minutes by taxi from the race track to the boat. I ran the race, and was starting to beat it to the taxi when something happened; you'd never guess what? The band struck up 'God save the King.' So, of course, I had to stand still as a post till they got through.

Then, of course, I was just about to leg it for the taxi but, what do you think happened then? Well, you'd hardly believe it, but the fellow who came in second to me was a Frenchman, so, of course, they had to start the Marseillaise, and there I was, tied like a post again! The taxi made it in great time. I took a healthy hop, step, and leap, and was on the edge of the wharf before it stopped. The boat was steadily moving out too far to jump. But a bit of a tidal wave threw it back a little. Then I flung my bags on to the wharf and jumped. I remember I tried to remember in the very act how a gazelle jumps. I felt like one, and I made it; just made it.

A newspaper correspondent who was in the car had said that the leap was fifteen feet, though Eric doubted that.

Occasionally he ran in special races against visiting international athletes. In 1929, he ran against Dr Otto Peltzer (1900–1970), German World record holder at 880 yards. He beat the German over 400 metres, but narrowly lost at 800m.

In the pavilion afterwards, Otto said in broken English, 'Eric, you will represent Britain in the next Olympic Games.'

'No, no, I'm too old.'

How old are you?'

'I'm twenty-seven.'

Otto roared with laughter:

'Too old? I am twenty-nine, and I will represent Germany at the next Games in 1932.' And he did.

'You train for 800 metres,' said the German, 'and you are the greatest man in the world at that distance.'

What greater praise could any sportsman wish for when he who gave it was world record holder for that same distance?

However, Eric never ran again in public after 1930, and so he never did run in the 1932 Games.

In 1932 when he was passing through Canada on his way back from his first home leave in Scotland, Eric was interviewed by a journalist. Their interview went something like this:

'Are you glad you gave your life to missionary work? Don't you miss the limelight, the rush, the frenzy, the cheers, the rich red wine of victory?'

To this came the telling reply:

'Oh well, of course it's natural for a chap to think over all that sometimes, but I'm glad I'm in the work I'm engaged in now. A fellow's life counts for more at this than the other. Not a corruptible crown, but an incorruptible, you know.'

Eric had many happy and fruitful years in the work of the T.A.C.C. However, there was a great change in 1929 when Eric's father's period of missionary service came to an end. He had served for thirty years faithfully. This meant two things for Eric. One was that he would have to find alternative accommodation, and the other was that he would see his family again only on rare visits home.

At first he shared a flat with other colleagues at the college. One man who shared the flat for a time after 1931 was the Agent for the National Bible Society of Scotland. His name was Donald McGavin. Naturally he got to know Eric well. His opinion of Eric was, therefore, one of personal experience. He was to say:

'Eric was not only one of nature's gentlemen, he was a perfect Christian gentleman, and therein is the secret of all that he was and did. His life was centred in Christ, and everything was done as to the Lord … Eric's life glorified God.'

However, not long after the departure of his family back to Scotland, things took a turn in Eric's personal life. He was up to that time, though still in his twenties, unmarried. Naturally he prayed about finding a like-minded wife. It happened that his eye was attracted to one young lady in the summer of 1929. Soon romance was in the air and his life was to change very seriously! Her name was Florence Mackenzie.

Love and Marriage

Florence was just a year older than Eric's brother, Ernest. She had been in the same class as Ernest at school. And she had been in Eric's Sunday School (since 1926). She was a daughter of missionary parents, Hugh and Agnes Mackenzie. They had returned to Tientsin in 1926 after a home leave. Hugh served the mission work of the United Church of Canada as co-ordinator of all the UCC mission work in North China. His wife had been appointed to Weihwei (Henan Province) for evangelistic work in 1910. She and Hugh had seven children, of which Florence (born in 1911) was the eldest.

Agnes remembered first meeting Eric, at the Union Church on their return to Tientsin in 1926. She said:

'I remember he was very unassuming, and so gentle in his manner.'

His acquaintance and friendship with Florence just grew over the years. By the time she was seventeen the acquaintance had blossomed into a romance. That was in the summer of 1929, when Florence was just a little short of her eighteenth birthday. Their courting was carried out with great propriety and they both knew that it would be some years before they married. For one thing Florence was committed to training as a nurse in Toronto, which was due to start in July 1930. She would be in Canada until early 1934. However, they were engaged before she left.

This came as a surprise to many. Of course everything was done very properly.

'I was naïve,' said Florence later, 'Eric had become such a part of the family that I just didn't notice anything. Of course I was desperately in love with him, but I just couldn't get over the fact that he wanted to marry me.'

She accepted immediately, of course! Eric told the story of the formal engagement in a letter to friends:

On May 12th [1930] there was a large gathering at Mr and Mrs MacKenzie's house. There were about 40 people present from the L.M.S. and the United Church of Canada. Just after tea had been served Mr MacKenzie announced the engagement of their eldest daughter, Florence – to ME. It was a very happy day indeed. After the announcement we adjourned to the tennis court where we watched and participated in several sets. Florence and I had to play one of the sets and we fortunately won. I think the other side must have arranged it like that as they thought we ought to win. Florence left for Canada a month later, via England. In Canada she hopes to take a nursing course which will last about three years. After my home leave [1931–2] I hope to return via Canada and if Florence's course is finished we will come out together.

What wasn't so well known was that when Florence first accepted his proposal of marriage, he immediately wrote to his mother and sister in Edinburgh asking them to get him a diamond ring with five diamonds. They promptly went to an Edinburgh jeweller, purchased a suitable ring and sent it out *post haste* to China. It was when it arrived that the formal official engagement party took place on May 12th!

Eric did return to Scotland for his first home leave at the end of August 1931. Such periods of leave normally were for a year after every six years of service – like a sabbatical. Only, it usually involved quite a round of meetings and deputation work arranged by the missionary society or supporting church.

Eric went on home leave across the Pacific and then across America to Toronto to see his fiancée and some of her family before continuing on to Scotland to see his own family who had taken a house in Edinburgh. He was sure to have an enthusiastic welcome wherever he went in Scotland. In some ways it wasn't much of a holiday, considering the speaking engagements he would have to address throughout the year.

It was strange going back to his old church – the Morningside Congregational Church – at Holy Corner. One of the purposes of his home leave was to take a year at the Scottish Congregational College with a view to being ordained to the Christian ministry.

There were great welcome home meetings organised for Eric in Edinburgh and Glasgow. All sorts of 'celebrities' in the world of sport, local government, the Universities and the Church were present. But Eric was a brave man. He wasn't intimidated by the occasions. In his usual dignified and gracious manner, he didn't court popularity. In the Edinburgh meeting at St George's West Church on 30th September he reminded Christians in the audience:

'We are all missionaries. We carry our religion with us, or we allow our religion to carry us. Wherever we go, we either bring people nearer to Christ, or we repel them from Christ.'

At a similar meeting in Glasgow, he was even more direct:

'Two of the great problems the Church has to face are betting and gambling and intemperance. These evils are sapping the energy of our young people, and the Church has to put up a united front against them, or they are bound to lose ground.'

Apparently he held 300 football fans spellbound with his honest and simple words.

Among the many meetings he addressed were some causes very close to his heart. On 8th March at St Andrew's Church, Edinburgh, there was a well-attended meeting of the Lord's Day Association of Scotland. That year there were several motions carried, including one from Eric Liddell on 'Sunday Games':

> *That this meeting is of opinion that the increasing use of*
> *the Lord's Day for games and recreations, however harmless*

in themselves, is detrimental to the highest interests of the youth of the country, as well as adding to the amount of unnecessary labour of other people; and calls on all young people's organisations to give full consideration to this aspect of the question.

No one was happier to see young people involved in healthy sports and recreations than Eric. As he saw it, however, God's Word was to be respected. A quiet Sabbath was for the advantage of young and old, especially if it was motivated by a concern for Christian public worship. There were also the benefits of bodily rest besides any religious involvement. Eric could see, however, that once respect for the Lord's Day was lost it would be difficult to retain anything of a 'day of rest'. Family life would then suffer.

In an address on 'Christ's Challenge to Youth' in Dundee, towards the end of his home leave in Scotland, he pleaded with his hearers:

'It is not sufficient to admire Christ; it is not sufficient to love Him. "For me to live is Christ," cried the Apostle. That is the spirit in which work for God is to be done.'

This was the spirit of the man.

On Wednesday, 22nd June, Eric was ordained to the ministry of the Congregational Union of Scotland. To Eric's joy D. P. Thomson, by then a Church of Scotland minister in Dunfermline, offered up the ordination prayer. A few days later he was on his way back to China – via Canada naturally!

The time seemed to fly between his return to Tientsin in the autumn of 1932 to his wedding year, 1934. Early in 1934, Florence returned from her nurses training in Toronto and plans were set for the wedding. Among other things, his house had to be licked into shape for his new bride! How excited he was to go to the port at Taku with his future father-in-law to pick up Florence on Monday, 5th March. The wedding was set for Tuesday, 27th March.

Naturally it was quite a wedding. A report of it appeared on the front page of the local *Tientsin and Peking Times* and *North China News*. A civil ceremony took place in the morning and then in the afternoon, a service at the Union Church. After the ceremony, a reception was held in the bride's parents' house attended by a large number of guests, though none of Eric's family could be present. Sadly, Eric's father had died just a few months before – in November 1933. He was now with the Lord he had served faithfully.

After the wedding celebrations, Eric and Florence went on honeymoon to Western Hill, Peiping. Eric and his bride settled down to life as husband and wife, for the present in the London Mission, Tientsin. It was a time of wonderful happiness for them both, and the beginning of a happy and fruitful married life.

In the providence of God it was to be all too short …

Change of Direction

'Congratulations! A little girl.'

'What's her name to be?'

'Patricia Margaret.'

To the delight of the family, the Church family and Eric and Florence, a baby girl was born to Eric and Florence in July 1935. It was a happy occasion – and a life-changing one!

However, already the Liddell family were faced with the possibility of a move from Tientsin. It was suggested that Eric be redeployed to country church and evangelistic work. This had already been on his mind. It had also been on the mind of the District Council of the LMS supervising the work in North China. The possibility of such a move was a motive behind the study he had undertaken on his home leave and in his seeking ordination to the ministry. The Council in June 1935 – just before Patricia was born – had suggested he go to help at Siaochang, where he had been brought up for his first five years. They were rather short-handed there, and it was felt that the T.A.C.C. had too large a share of the available staff.

Eric and Florence discussed this at Pei-Tai-Ho.

'It's so soon after we've set up home here, and we're just starting a family,' suggested Florence.

'Yes, but what would the Lord have us do?'

They made it a matter of prayer, and decided that they should not go for the suggested year-and-a-half, because Eric did not feel a definite call to give up educational work at that point. He also felt his Chinese needed improvement. So, unless it was a definite posting they would stay put in Tientsin meanwhile.

In January 1937, another daughter was born to Eric and Florence, Heather Jean. She had been due in December and Florence was all for naming her Carol. Eric, however, wanted a name to remind him of his native Scotland and plumped for 'Heather'. In the end they drew lots. Eric wrote out two slips and put them in a bag. He said that Florence should draw the name out. It was 'Heather'. Afterwards, Eric admitted he had put Heather on both slips! There was no falling-out, though, and Heather it was.

That summer, however, it was clear that Eric would have to consider going into country work at Siaochang, around 120 miles or so inland to the south-west of Tientsin. The hard thing about this move was that it would not be possible for Florence and the girls to be with him there. However, this was a decision made after much prayerful consideration. Eric felt that the Lord was calling him to that needy area of work. It would be a great loss to the Tientsin Church situation in general and the College life in particular.

However, where God calls He equips. This is what Eric was to find very clearly.

The one closest to him was to say of Eric:

'Of course his secret was his "Practice of the Presence of God." He spent much time in quiet, and all his decisions were made in the light of what he felt was God's will for him.'

There were two serious conflict issues involving China in the 1920s and 1930s. One was a Civil War between the Western-backed Nationalists and the Russian-backed Communists. This began in 1927 and rumbled on with various degrees of violence and disruption. That was bad enough, but then after July, 1937, there was war between China and Japan. Japan had a policy of military domination in the region. Only a few weeks before the end of the year, Eric, with his brother, Rob, reached Siaochang to commence their mission work. Eric's work was in district evangelism, and Rob was superintendent of the hospital there.

Eric gave his first reaction:

So this was Siaochang, the place I would be working at until my home leave [1939–40]. The first days were spent in language study, for up to then all my work had been in English. We couldn't very easily leave the compound and go into the district owing to the conditions both of the country and of travel, so our thoughts turned to the opportunities at our door. There were many refugees on the compound and it came to us to have a week of meetings mainly for our workers and those living on the premises.

Siaochang was a smallish village at the heart of the North China plain in South Hopei. It was the centre of church planting and evangelistic work under the London Missionary Society. Eric's father had laboured in that work at the time Eric was born there, thirty-five years earlier.

Eric quickly made an impression.

'Do you regret coming here for this work?' a nurse called who enquired of Eric.

'Never!' he quickly replied, 'I have more joy and freedom in this work than I have ever experienced before.'

He did, of course, miss his family. The work was arduous and increasingly dangerous. Whatever fame his sporting triumphs may have given him, this was real life. And it was one in which, with the Lord's help, he was making a difference in people's lives.

As far as Eric's work was concerned, a colleague wrote that:

Eric's methods in systematically visiting the churches, preparing plans, drawing maps, and holding regular conferences with the Chinese preachers, were never complicated, but simple, clear and direct, like his own character. In preaching he never expounded elaborate theories, but suggested the possibility of a 'way of life,' lived on a higher plane – to use his favourite expression – 'A God-controlled life.' In Siaochang our preachers, nurses and students hung on his words, and 'the common people heard him gladly'.

Experiences in the Country Areas

Eric had more than one narrow escape from real danger.

On one occasion he heard of a wounded Chinese man in a temple twenty miles from the Mission Hospital at Siaochang. He had been shot by the Japanese. Though very risky and dangerous to try to rescue the man, for fear of meeting the Japanese, Eric determined he would attempt to do it.

'Would you take us in your cart?' Eric asked a Chinese carter.

'Only if you go with me, Mr Li-Mu-Shi (Pastor Liddell),' came the nervous reply.

The carter duly started his journey, and Eric followed on bicycle a little later.

By evening the carter reached a village about three miles from the village near where the wounded man lay. Eric went on by bike to make arrangements with the head man of the village for the wounded man to be removed. The temple where he lay was 100 yards away. No home had been open to the man because if he was to be discovered by the Japanese, the home would be destroyed.

It was all very dangerous.

The man had lain in the temple for days. The Japanese soldiers were in the next village a mile or so away. Eric then returned to the village at which the carter had stopped, after telling the wounded man he would be back for him the next day.

That night Eric lay down, wrapped in his old sheepskin coat.

'What will I say to the Japanese if I meet them,' he thought to himself. He took out his Chinese New Testament and opened it at Luke 16. His eyes fell on verse 10: 'He that is faithful in that which is least, is faithful also in much and he that is unjust in the least is unjust in much.'

It was as if God said to him: 'Be honest and straight.'

He committed himself and the situation to the Lord, turned over, and went to sleep.

They started early next morning to make their way to where the wounded man was.

On the way as they passed through one village a man ushered them in to his home. The Japanese military passed by the village – just yards away. The Lord had preserved Eric.

They reached the temple where the wounded man was lying. They laid him on the cart and left.

On the way they heard of another wounded man a short distance away. They went to see. The head man of the village took them to one of the outhouses. In the dim light Eric could see that he had a dirty rag round his neck. He had been one of six men the Japanese had lined up for execution. The officer had drawn his sword and slashed him from the back of his neck to his mouth and left him for dead.

Though the cart was small, the injured man squeezed on and sat on the cart shafts as the party made their way the eighteen miles to the Mission Hospital.

It was dangerous. The circling round of a Japanese airplane overhead indicated that Japanese troops were nearby. However, at four in the afternoon they reached their destination. Sadly, the first man died. The other recovered, however, and in the course of time he was converted to Christ.

Later the same year, Eric had another scary experience in connection with his church work:

I am writing this after an eventful few days. Last Sunday we had planned to hold a big baptismal service for several nearby villages but, already the day before, we heard heavy gunfire in the distance and by breakfast time a scouting plane was circling overhead, so many from the outlying villages didn't turn up, rightly fearing that an attack was about to start. As I addressed those receiving baptism, two shells exploded outside with a terrific noise and there was silence for a moment before we were able to continue. I don't think any who were baptised that day will easily forget what happened. No one left after the service was over, so we just continued with hymns and witness to keep up our spirits. As there were no opposition forces here, truckloads of Japanese soldiers soon hurtled through the village gates and they searched every building in the place. Though they came into the church they left without causing any real damage, but in the evening, when everyone had gone home and was too frightened to come to evening service, the church door opened and in came the man who used to be the local opium addict, thanking and praising God. It seems that, having reached a living faith in Christ, he had then been arrested on a trumped-up charge but, unlike many others, he had been acquitted. Hurrying home he came to church straight away to give thanks for his deliverance, unaware of the terror we had all known earlier in the day. Feeling I had been given a congregation, I got on with the service!

Eric had a great care for the wellbeing of those among whom he moved in and around Siaochang, notwithstanding the dangers faced from bandits and soldiers. He cared for people's souls as well as for their general comfort. He preached outdoors and in. He encouraged his hearers to receive and follow Christ. He sought to train up native Chinese preachers. He entered into the joys and sorrows of the people. He cared enough, too, to warn of sinful lives and commend Christ as the way, the truth and the life.

He wrote at one point:

I think of another little girl who had been sold to a family, where she was made a slave. She was beaten and ill-treated so badly that she became very ill. Someone found her, and took her to a Christian hospital, where all the terrible treatment she had received was seen in the marked and dreadfully bruised body. At the hospital, everything was done that skill could do, and after months of careful nursing and medical treatment she was made well and strong. She too experienced how love found her, helped and healed her, and brought her new life. Jesus means us to pass on to others His love in deeds of kind thought, remembering that what is done for one of His little ones is done for Him.'

After all his labours for Christ in the field over eighteen months, Eric was ready for his second home leave, due in 1939. With Florence and his two young girls he left for Scotland via Canada in June. He intended to spend some time there and then travel on to Britain. However, Germany had invaded Czechoslovakia that March, and the international situation was deteriorating. Eric wondered if he could spend all his home leave in Canada before returning to China.

That would mean though that Eric would not see the family in the U.K. So leaving Florence and the girls in Canada, Eric travelled across the Atlantic to Britain in November. The situation was dangerous, but in this too he prayed the Lord for journeying safety.

The Dangers of War

By the time Eric left Canada to travel across the Atlantic to Britain in early November, 1939, war had been declared by Britain against Germany. Eric knew that there were deep clouds of uncertainty covering all his travelling as well as the future of the work in China. Travel was dangerous, but in God's goodness he arrived safe and well in the homeland.

Although it was now seven years since his last home leave, people in Scotland still remembered warmly one of their favourite sons and heroes.

'BACK FROM CHINA,' the newspaper headline stated: 'a little older, balding, more serious'!

For the next number of months, Eric fulfilled all his engagements for the London Missionary Society. He spoke of the Japanese threat and the warfare in China; the various difficulties encountered. Through the goodness of God they had been able to carry on their mission work.

Listening to Eric, one minister could not but admire Eric's evident care for people.

'I imagine it is really the explanation of a good deal of his popularity. He really cared for folk, and had the gift of understanding.'

At the end of March 1940, Florence and the girls joined him from Canada and they spent a short time together in Scotland before heading back to China. It was going to be an extremely risky trip. For now the ships crossing the Atlantic were frequently the targets of the German U-Boats. However, they went on with the conviction that if it was God's will, they would be safely preserved and if not, His will be done, they were in the Lord's hands.

The journey back was so eventful, it is worth giving Eric's lengthy description of all that happened:

> *We went on board at the scheduled time. There was a good bit of inspection. Cameras were taken from us and will be returned on landing. The boat has a number of children on board. I don't know how many, but I should say that at least half are children. It's a small boat, with a compliment of 300 passengers and crew. There are a few even younger than Heather, who was just 3 years old.*
>
> *We were in a convoy and had an escort. The convoy is a delightful sight. Can you imagine 50 ships? All going along together, not of course in single file, but in about five lines. It is magnificent. Most of the boats are cargo ones; any passenger ships are in the centre for greater protection.*
>
> *It wasn't until we were off the Irish Coast that the real excitement started. It was at 8.30 at night, when the children were asleep. We were hit by a torpedo. Whether it was a 'dud' and only the cap exploded, or whether it had expended its energy, having been fired from too great a distance, or had exploded right below us, we are not sure.*

I would say that we were actually hit, and that only the cap exploded, judging from the feel of our cabin. No alarm was given for us to go to the boats, but the signal for all boats to zigzag was given by ours.

The next night we lost one of our ships at the back of the convoy. The sea was choppy — a very difficult one to spot submarines in. The escort left us the next day. This was the hardest of all days. About 10 a.m., a small boat about a quarter of a mile from us was torpedoed, blew up, and sank in two minutes: they must have hit the engine boiler. We were on deck ready for the boats, and everyone zigzagged. About noon 'all clear' went and we turned to dinner. We had just started, and were halfway through the first course, when the alarm went again. Another boat torpedoed. It didn't sink. We heard later that it was able to get along. Whether it turned back or tried to carry on, I don't know.

We were still in convoy, but not escorted now. By teatime they decided it was too dangerous going on in convoy, so we broke it and each put on full steam ahead, some going north and others south. It was a tense time right up to the next morning. At 6 p.m. word came through by wireless that the ship which had been sailing next to us, about 200 yards off, for the last two days had been torpedoed. Ten minutes later, another; and at 9 o'clock at night we heard that a submarine had risen to the surface and was being engaged by one of the convoy in a running fight.

The ship was running at full speed, far above its average. All night, people slept in their clothes, with lifebelts ready. The next day the tension eased; we were out of range of the ordinary submarines; only an ocean-going one could come so far, and there were few of these. The greater speed in the heavy sea caused numbers to be seasick again. Since then it has been calmer. No excitement; we have had enough for one trip. The escort shouldn't have left for another day at least. We must just have been followed up by 'subs' and when they saw the escort gone they enjoyed themselves.

In some ways, it was a miracle that Eric and family ever got back to China on that trip. They were conscious of the divine protection. The young daughters at least were largely unaware of what was happening and were not afraid.

He continued the story in a letter to his mother:

Sunday, August 18th. The weather was foggy, but not a heavy fog. The captain was on the bridge all day, so that there was no service in the morning. Late in the day someone heard that I was a minister, and asked if I would be willing to conduct a service. I only had my sports coat and flannels, but they didn't mind. At 8.30 we had a service in the 1st class lounge. It was in a form of thanksgiving for our escape. We undressed that night and had a good sleep.

The boat entered harbour in Canada the following Friday and Eric and the family had a welcome break of ten days in Toronto, before going on to China via Vancouver, arriving at Tientsin by the end of October.

Soon Eric was back at work in Siaochang. He had returned, however, to an increasingly dangerous situation.

Closing Scenes of Missionary Service

By the time Eric returned to the country work around Siaochang, it was a garrisoned village. Rob and his family had left China by now, due to one of Rob's children needing urgent medical attention in the U.K. A high wall surrounded the south village, so that Eric could say:

> As I look out of my bedroom window in the east house, the south village looks like one of the outposts of the Empire. The last few days we have watched rather depressed and dejected men going out on forced labour, to prepare a motor road to pass to the east of Siaochang.

The Chinese country and farming folk were suffering and Eric was concerned to help them, and give them the love and hope of the gospel. When the Japanese were near most locals were too scared to come out to meetings. Eric always did what he could in conducting worship and prayers and caring for his flock. The sort of situation he faced was well described by Eric in one of his letters. It involved what happened following a wedding at a weekend:

> I stayed over on Sunday, taking the service and chatting with the people. I should have returned that day, but the cart I was expecting did not arrive till nightfall. It had

> *been delayed by the 8th Army [Communist Chinese], who*
> *were stopping the moving of all the carts. On our return*
> *journey today there was little of incident except at one*
> *point. The enemy must have taken us for the 8th Army and*
> *fired two shots. We just got off our bikes and stayed still*
> *till they realised their mistake, and then we went on.*

Things worsened. In February 1941, the Japanese closed down the hospital and foreign residences, sealed the properties and took all the keys of the various buildings from the superintendent. The compound at Siaochang was thus closed and the missionaries finally were forced to abandon the work there. Eric cycled alongside the last cart that drew out of the compound. It was a sad moment for Eric. He had such happy memories of that place; memories of early happy childhood days, days of youthful innocence. He had memories of his father's work there, and then his own more recently together with his brother, Rob. Yet the Lord had His purpose in this and Eric believed that there would yet be fruit from the work and prayers of those who had so faithfully laboured for Jesus and the gospel in Siaochang.

On 18th February, everyone was back in Tientsin. A cable was sent to London:

Siaochang safely evacuated …

That spring Eric and Florence came to realise that conditions were worsening in Tientsin itself. It was clear that soon all foreign missionaries would be interned by the Japanese.

'Look, Florence,' said Eric, 'things are getting really bad, and I think it would be best if you went to Canada with the girls, especially since you're expecting another baby. I would hate for anything to happen to you here. I'll join you there when this business is over, Lord willing.'

'There seems to be little choice.'

That June the whole family set off for Japan with a view to Florence and the girls catching a boat there across the Pacific. The family had four days before they boarded *The Nita Maru*. Sadly, daddy had to leave them on the boat before it set sail. He offered up a prayer for their safety and with many kisses and hugs took his leave of them.

They trusted in the Lord that it may be His will that they be reunited. In His providence and mysterious purpose that was not to be. This was the last glimpse Florence, Patricia and Heather were to get of Eric in this world.

On 17th September 1941, another daughter was born to Florence and Eric. Nancy Maureen was born in Toronto. Eric, when he heard, was absolutely elated. Even in the midst of distress and danger, there was joy in the goodness of the Lord.

Eric went back to Tientsin where he continued to live and do what he could in the interests of the gospel of Christ as long as it was possible. At first he shared a flat with an old colleague at the T.A.C.C. It was a happy arrangement until the college was closed by the Japanese.

The Japanese bombed Pearl Harbour in December 1941. This brought America into the War. As a result, the position of the 'enemy aliens' in Japanese-occupied China became exposed, to say the least.

During this time Eric was very restricted in the work he could do. It seemed to be only a matter of time before the remaining westerners would be taken into captivity by the Japanese. That in fact happened fourteen months later, in March 1943.

Until then Eric occupied himself in several ways. There was still church work in the Union Church where Eric often took services and helped in other aspects of the work there. He was also very active in helping those who had various special needs. Among the numerous young people still around, Eric would play sports with them as opportunity allowed. The Christian communities in Tientsin in those days were very mutually supportive of one another, notwithstanding the obvious hardships.

An important factor in Eric's life was his early morning hour of prayer and communion with the Lord, a discipline he sought to keep up in all circumstances. In such hard times this was a source of great strength.

Given the disruption of the normal avenues of missionary service, Eric settled down, among other things, to produce for Union Church a book of *Prayers* for *Daily Use*. The idea of such a book was not that these would take the place of private devotions. They were brought together to help in forming thoughts about prayer and bring out thoughts that would be helpful for all Christian life. For example, in one place he speaks of 'The Key to Knowing God'. He speaks of the place of *obedience*:

> *One word stands out above all others as the key to knowing God, to having His peace and assurance in your heart; it is obedience.*
>
> *Obedience to God's Will is the secret of spiritual knowledge and insight. It is not willingness to know, but willingness to do (obey) God's Will that brings certainty. 'If any man will do [obey] His Will, he shall know of the doctrine, whether it be of God, or, whether I speak of Myself'. (John 7:17) ...*
>
> *Obedience is the secret of being conscious that God guides you personally.*
>
> *Every Christian should live a God-guided life. If you are not guided by God you will be guided by something else. The Christian that hasn't the sense of guidance in his life is missing something vital.*
>
> *To obey God's Will was like food to Jesus, refreshing His mind, body and spirit. 'My meat is to do the will of Him that sent me' (John 4:34). We can all have the same experience if we make God's will the dominant purpose in our lives.*
>
> *Take obedience with you into your time of prayer and meditation, for you will know as much of God, and only as much of God, as you are willing to put into practice. There is a great deal of truth in the hymn 'Trust and obey'.*

> *When we walk with the Lord,*
> *In the light of His Word,*
> *What a glory He sheds on your way!*
> *While we do his good will,*
> *He abides with us still,*
> *And with all who will trust and obey.*

Also in the year before his internment Eric worked on a manual called: *A Manual of Christian Discipleship*. This book was afterwards published in Britain and America under the title *The Disciplines of the Christian Life*. In an explanation of the purpose of this book Eric wrote:

> *In this book I am attempting to do three things:*
>
> 1. *To place before people the limited amount of Christian knowledge that every Christian should have;*
> 2. *To help people apply their knowledge to daily life; to live according to the light they have;*
> 3. *To develop the devotional life so as to create basic Christian thinking on subjects of conduct, action, outlook, and attitudes.*
>
> *The Christian life should be a life of growth. I believe the secret of growth is to develop the devotional life.*
>
> *This involves setting aside each day a time for prayer and Bible study.*

On 12th March, 1943 the British and American residents and other 'enemy nationals' in Tientsin were told that they were to go to the Civil Assembly Centre at Weihsien in Shantung Province. Eric was in the last of the groups to go there, on 30th March. The internees were only allowed to take four pieces of luggage each. One had to be bedding and the other three trunks or boxes. Two suitcases could also be carried as hand luggage on the journey.

The journey by rail from Tientsin was some 400 miles to the South East. The Internment camp was for Civil Internees; it was not a 'Prisoner of War' Camp, though the Chinese later described it in that way. Having said that, it would be a cramped and uncomfortable situation with very limited rations. All in all, it would be a situation not easily endured. But many of the internees would be professing Christians and the very fact of such fellowship would sustain the spirits of many in a discouraging situation. However, tensions were sure to arise, given the mix of people herded into such a relatively confined space.

For Eric, and no doubt for many other Christians, such a situation was an opportunity to show the power and reality of a living Christian faith and hope, in the face of extreme hardness and adversity.

Captivity

The 400 miles rail journey from Tientsin to Weihsien was a very different one from the great Trans-Siberian rail journey that had brought Eric to China sixteen years earlier. He had the same joy of the Lord in his heart, but there was sadness at the suspension of the Christian mission work, the hardships experienced by the native Chinese and the foreign missionaries. As well as that, Eric had been separated from his wife and family.

Eric was captain in charge of the third group that was to make its way to the Internment Camp at Weihsien. The third group of men, women and children of various nationalities assembled in Tientsin at 7.30 in the evening of 30th March, 1943 and under Japanese guard moved off at 9 o'clock for the station. The streets were lined with sympathetic silent crowds, mostly Chinese. When they reached the train, the internees took their allotted places and the train moved off a little before midnight.

It was a tiring journey. Few slept. At 10.30 the next morning there was a change of trains at Tsinan (Capital of Shantung Province). The group finally arrived at Weihsien at twenty to four in the afternoon.

A tired group of rather bedraggled folk made their weary way by an assortment of trucks and buses to the 'Civil Assembly Centre'. There they gathered in the Athletic Ground for directions about accommodation quarters.

The premises used by the Japanese consisted of the compound of the American Presbyterian Mission about a couple of miles from the city of Weihsien. It was, therefore, quite compact and at the same time pretty isolated. It was ideal for an internment situation. It was fairly easily 'controlled' by having a perimeter that could be made secure by barbed wire, lights and guard towers. It had a fair amount of facilities too. It had been a sort of self-contained village, in which there had been five departments – a Men's Theological School and a Women's Bible Training School; Boys' and Girls' Middle Schools, and a fine hospital. This meant that there was accommodation, schooling facilities, games areas, dining areas and a hospital as well. However, it was not going to be comfortable because the number of internees placed in the compound was so great.

By the time the third contingent arrived that cold March morning, the complement of the camp was near 1,800. Bearing in mind the fact that the Japanese had taken over the best accommodation, and that there were only 400 individual rooms on the compound, it may easily be recognised how cramped the available space was.

Whatever the restrictions, this was life for the time being for the unhappy internees and they had to make the best of it. No doubt it was a great blessing from the Lord, that among the internees were so many Christian believers, but there were also many who had no time for religion and no faith in Christ. However, despite the diversity of backgrounds there was a good degree of co-operation in the overall running of the camp.

Among the internees were some aged missionary workers including Herbert Hudson Taylor, son of the founder of the China Inland Mission, J. Hudson Taylor. Herbert at the time was in his early 80s. Also with him was a son, William Taylor, and his wife and four children. William was the third generation of Taylors involved in mission work in China.

Another internee was the Rev John Parker. He was 82 when Eric arrived at the camp. Parker had been Eric's father's predecessor in the work in Mongolia with the London Missionary Society. Sadly, he died in the camp in June 1944. Herbert Taylor, though, survived and lived on till 1950.

As far as accommodation went, the single and unattached were placed in dormitories and the married couples and children in individual rooms, of which there were many in the camp. At first Eric was in one of these 13 feet by 9 feet rooms, sharing with LMS colleagues Revs Edwin Davies and Joe McChesney-Clark, an Australian.

One can imagine how in such cramped accommodation room mates get to know one another fairly well. The wife of one of Eric's room mates, during the time in the camp, was to tell of the impression he made, as told by her husband:

Every morning about 6 a.m., with curtains tightly drawn to keep in the shining of our peanut oil lamp, lest the prowling sentries should think someone was trying to escape, he used to climb out of his top bunk, past the sleeping forms of his dormitory mates. Then, at the small Chinese table, the two men would sit close together with the light just enough to illumine their Bibles and notebooks. Silently they read, prayed, thought about the day's duties, noted what should be done. Eric was a man of prayer not only at set times – though he did not like to miss a Prayer Meeting or Communion service when such could be arranged. He talked to God all the time, naturally, as one can who enters the 'School of prayer' to learn this way of inner discipline. He seemed to have no weighty mental problems: his life was grounded in God, in faith, and in trust.

This was both the secret of a godly life, as well as an explanation of effective witness for Christ.

Initially, things were very basic as the camp had been plundered of furniture and other items before the internees arrived. Sanitation was also poor. However, things improved a bit as time went on. Tremendous effort was put into the camp organisation. Different 'departments' were set up, each with its own committee and leadership. There were nine in all:

1. Discipline
2. Education, Entertainment and Athletics
3. Employment
4. Engineering and Repairs
5. Finance
6. General Affairs
7. Medical
8. Quarters and Accommodation
9. Supplies

There was also a Christian Fellowship of the Protestant Churches, Women's Auxiliary, and Homes Committee (to help women in their homes). One of the important features of camp life would be to try to encourage as normal a life as possible. So, there was a concern for a whole range of 'normal' activities like work (at least three hours a day!), school, entertainments, sports, crafts and the like. An issue would be internal friction that would most likely arise from boredom. There was also the point that there was a range of nationalities and a mix of people who were religious and irreligious. That was obviously an issue with the observance of the Lord 's Day.

With so many ministers and missionaries in the camp, the spiritual aspects of camp life were well catered for. There were many services, prayer meetings and Bible classes. Each Sunday there were two Protestant services in the compound church. One was at 11 a.m. and another at 5 o'clock, with a Sunday School service in between times. The Salvation Army held a public meeting on Thursday evenings and otherwise made their presence felt though their band-playing at other times. Eric frequently took services and prayer meetings, and taught Bible Class on Sundays.

Eric played a full part in the camp life. He acted as a teacher of maths and science, and was in charge of sports. He also acted as warden of two blocks, buildings housing 230 single and unattached men, women, boys and girls. This involved dealing with problems, helping the needy, keeping up discipline and morale, and getting them all out to roll-calls every morning and evening. It was all very positive; the education involving examinations which it was hoped would afterwards earn certificates from Education authorities 'back home'.

Eric was one of the General Committee of the Protestant Christian Fellowship in the camp that oversaw the Christian activities. He had special concern for the youth work. He was always enormously popular with the young people in the camp. It was a tough task, given the situation. However, his devotion to the Lord made a deep impression on all these young people whose lives had been so disrupted by events. Eric, though, set about it all with his customary cheerfulness and spiritual concern.

As far as camp life was concerned, the organisation of education was one thing. Though there were many people well able to teach across a wide range of subjects, some of what was taught had to be improvised because of a lack of equipment. There was education not only for the young, but also for adults. There was, after all, a lot of time to fill. Entertainment, sport, and of course religious exercises assumed great importance. There were weekly entertainments on Fridays and Saturdays. Programmes were put on with classical music, oratorios, Mozart, Mendelssohn as well as more popular items. Quiz evenings, children's concerts and plays were organised as well as Boy Scout and Girl Guide troops.

The fairly large athletic ground gave opportunity for various sports. One young man in the camp, who later became a missionary himself, left a great story about an Annual Games meeting in August 1944.

The sports day on the playing field was a speck of glitter in the dull monotony of camp life … Then, as the veterans' race prepared to start, a hush distilled over the crowd. Our eyes shifted to the chairman of the Camp Recreation Committee, who was starting well behind the others as a voluntary handicap.

'He can never make up that distance!' gasped a boy beside me.

'He can too! He will, just wait!' I hissed back.

Down the track they came. Middle-aged runners, weakened by the rigours and poor food of camp life, puffed and panted their way onward in response to our cheers.

Then, unbelievably, the runner in rear position surged powerfully forward, arms flailing wildly, head thrown back. Out ahead now, he pushed for the finish line. He did it! One great, wild chorus of cheers nearly drowned out the judge's voice,

'Eric Liddell wins the veterans' event!'

'I knew he could do it! He always wins!'

We basked in the aura of Olympic glory as – cheering, chanting, chattering – we surrounded our hero.

Besides his teaching work, Eric took responsibility for organising all the games. He arranged for the Americans to run a series of baseball matches. Though they requested Sunday games, Eric stuck to his principles and took no responsibility for such events on Sunday. There were no formal games at all encouraged on Sundays. As someone put it: 'His old principle stood unchanged and all respected him for it, including those who defied it!'

Only in one instance did Eric relent. Some Sundays a group of young people, not willing to respect the Lord's Day, organised games among themselves. Without oversight one week it broke out into fighting. Eric decided that disruption must be restrained and so he 'kept order' in overseeing such impromptu Sunday activities. He felt that he had to limit the damage and stop the disturbance of others. It was a tough call and it seems that it troubled Eric not a little.

Home Straight

'Don't stare now, but the man coming towards us is Eric Liddell.'

So whispered one internee to a newcomer.

Eric was in demand, and greatly loved throughout the camp. He carried a fair load of work as a result. One internee who arrived later than the others came wearily into the camp after travelling for hours. This is what he said about his first encounter with Eric:

> I was too limp to connect the oncoming stranger with the 'well-known' Olympic athlete of some years before, but I glanced aside to note the man on the path. He was not very tall, rather thin, very bronzed with the sun and air. He was wearing the most comical shirt I had ever seen, though I was to get quite accustomed to similar garments in that place. It was made, I learned later, from a pair of Mrs Liddell's curtains. But what struck me most about him was his very ordinary appearance. He didn't look like a famous athlete, or rather he didn't look as if he thought of himself as one. That, I came to know in time, was one of the secrets of his amazing life. He was surely the most modest man who ever breathed.

Eric made an impression among the young people. One of them was to write later:

> *Two men have made a profound and lasting impression on my life – my father, who died in China, aged 53, and Eric Liddell, who died at 43. Both were outstanding in their humility, utter selflessness and supreme devotion to Christ, whom they served 'faithful unto death.' My constant prayer is that I may be worthy of them and have grace to follow their example.'*

To the young people he was 'Uncle Eric'. But to young and old alike he was selfless in his help and care. One of his fellow prisoners wrote:

> *I met Eric for the first time in Weihsien Internment Camp in 1943 when I was eighteen years of age. At a special evangelistic rally he spoke of the story of the rich young ruler, showing us in a way I shall never forget the cost of Christian discipleship. I was immediately impressed with his humility and directness of speech. This was apparent not only at the religious meetings, but also as a coach or referee on the playing field or in the lecture hall.*

As far as the conditions in the camp were concerned, Eric would dismiss them with a twinkle in his eye. He was one of those people who would do anything for anyone. He was famous for it in the camp. Whether it was trying to sort out people's anxieties, or distributing Red Cross parcels, or carrying things for the elderly or infirm.

He sought to point people to what the gospel offered to all. He was able to endure the hardships because he lived like the apostle: 'I have learned in whatever state I am, to be content: I know how to be abased, and I know how to abound. Everywhere and in all things I have learned both to be full and to be hungry, both to abound and to suffer need. I can do all things through Christ who strengthens me' (Philippians 4:11-13).

Eric naturally wrote often to his dear wife and family. These were only 'snatches' of camp life and of his feelings as they would be twenty-five or 100 words only.

> *I'm not losing weight and feel fit, don't worry. The Lord is good.*

The truth was that conditions deteriorated in the camp as time went on, notably towards the end of 1944. The poor nutrition and the burdens that Eric bore took their toll on him, fit though he appeared to be. No one would have thought that he of all people would suffer a fatal condition. A decline in Eric's health became evident in the autumn of 1944. It was at this time, in September 1944, that Eric's mother passed away in Edinburgh. It is more than likely that he never learned of this.

As 1945 dawned in the camp, Eric spoke of suffering from agonising headaches. He used to lie with bandaged eyes just looking for quiet. Something was seriously wrong and there were no adequate medical services. There was a basic service from doctors and nurses among the internees and they certainly did their very best in the circumstances, but they were limited in what they could do. At any rate things became so bad for him that he was put into the hospital. On Sunday, 11 February 1945, Eric had a slight stroke in hospital.

Few visitors were allowed in hospital, but those who did visit Eric invariably went away cheered. Eric was, however, distressed about his family whom he missed so much. He hadn't even met his youngest daughter, Maureen.

After the better part of a month, Eric seemed to rally and was able to get out and about, though he still suffered considerably with head pains.

In reply to the enquiry: 'Is your head any better?' he would answer:

'To answer that question I should require to know what is going on inside my head.'

It was clear, though, that something was seriously wrong. He was now so thin and ill. The doctor thought he may have had a nervous breakdown. However, things did not improve. The doctors came to suspect a brain tumour.

The wife of one of Eric's colleagues, a cook in the hospital kitchen, asked him:

'Have you heard from Flo?'

'Oh, yes,' he replied, telling her the news.

She thought him tired and slow in his speaking.

'You should be resting more.'

'No,' said Eric, 'I must just get my walking legs again.'

But that was the very day the Lord took him. His faltering steps were taking him to the camp Post Office where he was to post the very last letter he would write to his dear wife. For it was that day, 21st February 1945, that he wrote to Florence:

Was carrying too much responsibility. Am much better after a month in hospital. Doctor suggests changing my work. Giving up teaching and athletics and taking up physical work like baking ... A good change. Keep me in touch with the news. Enjoying comfort and parcels. Special love to you and the children. – Eric.

That evening he was back in hospital. He was clearly seriously ill and was moved to a ward on his own. A colleague, Annie Buchan, was with him at the end. Annie had been matron in the Siaochang Hospital when Eric and Rob Liddell had been working there together. She was a Scots lass from Peterhead, and a spiritually-minded soul. She wrote to D. P. Thomson afterwards:

I was with him when he died. The last words he said to me were, 'Annie, it is surrender.' He then lapsed into a coma, and about half past nine that evening he went peacefully home.

That was a wonderful way to describe the death of a Christian: 'went peacefully home'. As the old *Catechism* answer put it: At death the souls of believers are made perfect in holiness and do immediately pass into glory, and their bodies, being still united to Christ rest in the grave till the resurrection. Eric's hope was in Christ for time, in death, and for eternity.

In those last weeks, when he was lying so ill on his hospital bed, the Salvation Army band as usual played various hymn tunes for the encouragement of the patients. One of these was the tune *Finlandia*, so closely associated with the hymn, 'Be still, my soul: the Lord is on thy side.' It was well known to Eric. One can well imagine how his thoughts must have dwelt then on the verse that was so encouraging to the Christian:

> *Be still, my soul: the hour is hastening on*
> *When we shall be forever with the Lord,*
> *When disappointment, grief, and fear are gone,*
> *Sorrow forgot, love's purest joys restored.*
> *Be still my soul: when change and tears are past,*
> *All safe and blessed we shall meet at last.*

He believed in the truth of this, and for him the promise of Jesus surely applied which said: 'Blessed *are* the dead who die in the Lord from now on. Yes,' says the Spirit, 'that they may rest from their labours, and their works follow them' (Revelation 12:13).

Sweet Sorrow

The news of Eric's sudden passing went round the camp like wildfire. They all found it hard to take in.

'He was such a young and fit man.'

'How could he be taken in such a way?'

But the Christian does not mourn as those who do not have hope. Because the soul of the person who dies with a living faith in Christ has gone to be with the Lord. Those who are left feel it though. Eric made such an impact on people's lives for good in the camp, that it was sure that he would be greatly missed.

'The earth was white with snow next morning when we heard the news,' said one fellow internee. 'I walked across the camp, in its glittering whiteness, and eternal realities were the more real that day.'

An autopsy was carried out the morning after Eric's passing. It showed that he had been suffering from an inoperable tumour on the left side of his brain. This was the cause of the fatal brain haemorrhage to which he had finally succumbed.

Three days after Eric's passing, a short service was held. It was Saturday, 24th February, and a huge crowd pressed in and around the assembly hall of the camp. The service was conducted by a senior LMS missionary, the Rev Arnold Bryson. It was a solemn occasion, and yet not unmixed with joy at the passing of a saint of God. Among other things, Mr Bryson was to say:

> *Yesterday a man said to me, 'Of all the men I have known, Eric Liddell was one in whose character and life the spirit of Jesus Christ was pre-eminently manifested.' ...What was the secret of his consecrated life and far-reaching influence? Absolute surrender to God's will as revealed in Jesus Christ. His was a God-controlled life and he followed his Master and Lord with a devotion that never flagged and with an intensity of purpose that made men see both the reality and power of true religion. With St. Paul, Eric could say, 'I live, yet not I, but Christ liveth in me.' ...*

After the service there was a simple interment in the cemetery, within the bounds of the camp. There his body was laid to rest alongside others who had died in the camp. Many tears were shed. The grave was marked by a simple cross on which his name had been inscribed in black boot polish.

A Memorial service was held in the camp on 3rd March. This was led by a former tutor at Eltham and colleague at the Anglo-Chinese College in Tientsin, the Rev A.P. Cullen. Several others spoke of various phases of Eric's life. Fitting tribute was paid to a 'Mr Greatheart'.

One of the most moving of tributes to Eric came from a diary kept by an internee to record impressions and reflections of camp life. This is what the diarist was to write on the day of Eric's funeral:

He was not particularly clever, and not conspicuously able,
but he was good. He was naturally reserved and tended to
live in a world of his own, but he gave of himself unstintedly.
His reserve did not prevent him from mixing with everybody
and being known by everybody, but he always shrank from
revealing his deepest needs and distresses, so that whilst he
bore the burdens of many, very few could help bear his.

His fame as an athlete helped him a good deal. He
certainly didn't look like a great runner, but the fact that
he had been one gave him a self-confidence that men of
his type don't often have. He wasn't a great leader, or an
inspired thinker, but he knew what he ought to do, and he
did it. He was a true disciple of the Master and worthy of
the highest of places amongst the saints gathered in the
Church triumphant. We have lost of our best, but we have
gained a fragrant memory.

The value of this testimony to Eric's character lies in
the fact that it was not written for the general public
and it has the virtue of real honesty. Eric was a saint
in the sense that he was a true Christian believer.
However, like all true believers he had to contend
with limitations. He did, however, make the best of
what the Lord had given him by way of talents and
opportunities. In this Eric always was and will ever
remain a good 'role-model' for all who would seek to
be faithful to the Master, the Lord Jesus Christ.

As one might imagine, when the news of Eric's
passing finally came to Florence and his girls in
Toronto it came as a numbing shock. It was not until
2nd May, 1945 that Florence finally received the sad

news. It was not easy to come to terms with. There were so many questions. Yet she did come to thank the Lord for the happy time she had enjoyed in marriage to Eric and to resign herself to the will of the One who does all things well.

A Grim Outcome?

I ask myself the question, as I'm sure you do, 'Why should such a fruitful life of such a good man in his prime be cut short?'

There is no easy answer. The Apostle Paul felt that dilemma: 'For to me, to live *is* Christ, and to die *is* gain' (Philippians 1:21). Like Paul, Eric knew that for the Christian to depart and be with Christ was 'far better' (v. 23). The final answer is that it pleases the Lord in His good purpose, and all things work together for good to those who love Him and are the called according to His purpose (Romans 8:28).

It was not long after Eric's passing that the camp was liberated. Just a few months. On 17th August, 1945 the American forces moved in and liberated the Weihsien Camp. Victory over Japan had been achieved by the surrender of the Japanese two days earlier. There was some attempt afterwards to return to 'normality' and for the missionaries to resume their Christian work. That was to be short-lived. China was soon in the throws of another revolution which was to have a profound affect on Christian missionary work there. In the post-War struggles for power between Nationalists and Communists, the Communists led by

Mao Tse-tung prevailed. After Mao's rise to power in 1949, all Christian missionary work effectively came to an end, missions were closed and foreign missionaries were expelled. State atheism was to prevail.

On the face of it, this seemed a grim outcome. Much mission work had been undertaken in China and now it was to end. As far as the Protestant missions were concerned, some of this had been Church-sponsored and in the 20th century had been undermined by a departure in the Western Churches from the authority of the Bible.

However, the work done through a consistent gospel approach, following such pioneer missionaries as William Chalmers Burns, J. Hudson Taylor, and James Gilmour, would produce fruit for the Saviour despite Government disapproval after 1949. We may believe that the work done by such as the Liddells, father and sons, was 'not in vain in the Lord'.

There is good evidence for this. There have been reports of a growing Christian presence in China. There may be as many as 100 million professing Christians today in China, a scale of things unimagined by missionaries like Eric Liddell and his father.

In 2008, the Olympic Games were held in Beijing. Eric Liddell's story of Olympic success, birth on Chinese soil, and Christian mission work in China presented an opportunity to point out the good influence and traditions of Christianity in China's history.

I had an opportunity to visit North China during the Games and, in meetings with various state officials in connection with Eric Liddell, it was clear that he and other missionaries, in the period before 1949, were highly respected. To these men Eric was a 'hero'. Even the hardest anti-Christian Communist had to concede that behind so much Christian missionary work was a real concern for the wellbeing of the Chinese people. It was a great pleasure to have my biography of Eric, *Running the Race*, translated into simplified Chinese and published and distributed in China in 2008 with the approval of the state authorities and censors.

It does appear, then, that there has been fruit for Christ from all the mission work earnestly and prayerfully carried out in that great land. This is what one would expect given what the Word of God teaches: 'For as the rain comes down, and the snow from heaven, and do not return there, but water the earth, and make it bring forth and bud, that it may give seed to the sower and bread to the eater, so shall my word be that goes forth from my mouth; it shall not return to me void, but it shall accomplish what I please, and it shall prosper *in the thing* for which I sent it' (Isaiah 55:10-11).

A Life Well Remembered

Eric Liddell's life was in some ways extraordinary. Yet in many ways it was ordinary. It was certainly a life that touched many people in his own day and afterwards. And he was well remembered. He is still well remembered.

When it was suggested that there should be a *Scottish Sports Hall of Fame* and a poll was taken of interested parties about who might initially be included, top of the poll was Eric Liddell. More than sixty-five years after his death and nearly eighty since his Olympic triumph, he was still remembered as one of Scotland's greatest athletes. He was one of the first fifty inducted to the Hall on 30th November, 2002.

In 2009, a programme was devised for Scottish Television entitled *The Greatest Scot*. There were several categories including sport in which names were put forward by a specially selected panel of 'experts'. Included among them was Eric Liddell. He wasn't finally selected as the 'Greatest Scot'. He would not likely have been at all impressed by such a programme and of his own name being put forward for it. However, it did show in just how high a regard he has continued to be held, even though he was a

Christian, something not at all well understood in recent times in Britain.

Among the many ways in which Eric has been remembered in recent times, has been through the Oscar-winning film *Chariots of Fire*. This film won an Oscar for best picture in 1981 and is still rated as one of the very best sporting films ever made. In the late 1970s, an eminent film producer named David Puttnam was unwell and recuperating in the house of a friend. He found a copy of a book on the history of the Olympic Games and was taken by the successes of British athletes at the 1924 Games in Paris. Harold Abrahams (100m), Eric Liddell (400m) were champions of very different backgrounds. Puttnam could see the possibilities of a good film bringing out social issues, sporting action and heroism.

The film was not done with a view to being a great success, yet it turned out to be exactly that. The action was good; the photography was great (there was no computer enhanced imaging), the music was wonderful, and the acting – by non-athletes and involving a little known cast of actors – was superb. A 'hit' any day.

Eric himself would have been amazed at the interest in what he had done in his life, so too were his widow, daughters and other family members. *Chariots of Fire* came as a complete surprise to them. They had no idea there was such an interest in his life.

Among other things the film established the memory of Eric Liddell firmly in the minds of the public. He comes over well as a 'muscular Christian'; a man of quiet principle and great heart. Though many of the details are not true to real life in the film, the impression given of the athletes and of the era were good. Eric Liddell is portrayed well. His faith, modesty, sportsmanship and determination are well presented.

After news of his passing became known in 1945, there was a real concern to do something by which he would be remembered. Eric's great friend and mentor, D. P. Thomson, produced a short biography and helped launch an 'Eric Liddell Fund' to keep fresh his memory in Scotland (and beyond).

The purpose of the fund was four-fold:

- To provide in some measure for the education and nurture of Eric Liddell's daughters;
- To endow a Missionary Scholarship at Edinburgh University;
- To institute a Challenge Trophy for Amateur Athletics in Scotland; and,
- To set up a suitable Memorial in North China. The appeal was made in the sum of £10,000.

How much was finally raised is not now known, though of these aims only two were secured: help for the education of the Liddell girls, and the institution of an Eric Liddell Trophy, to be presented annually for the best performance at the Scottish Schools Athletic

Association Championships. The Fund also published a forty-page booklet by D. P. Thomson on Eric's life up to the time he went to China. This became a 'bestseller' in the late 1940s.

At Weifang on Sunday, 9th June 1991 there was a celebration at the garden of remembrance on the site of the Internment Camp, where David Michell had been in 1985. This time there was a ceremony to mark the setting up of the *Eric Liddell Foundation*, a trust formed to bring Chinese, Hong Kong and British athletes together for sports and 'character building education'.

In that quiet corner of the Number Two Middle School grounds where the garden had been built, a seven-foot high slab of red granite from the Isle of Mull was unveiled. Gold characters on the front of the stone told the bare details of Liddell's life in English and Chinese. On the back was a text: 'They shall mount up with wings as eagles. They shall run and not be weary' (Isaiah 40:31). This was subsequently moved to a site beside the former Shadyside Hospital, one of the last remaining buildings of the original compound.

There have been many other ways in which Eric's memory has been kept fresh. There is 'The Eric Liddell Centre' established in 1992 at Edinburgh's Holy Corner in the Morningside area of the city and just opposite the Congregational Church of which Eric Liddell had been a member in the 1920s. The purpose of the Centre is both social and spiritual. It supports caring and educational projects, and provides a coffee shop, conference facilities and other services of a broadly Christian nature.

Eltham College did not forget arguably their most famous son. In June 1996, they established a state-of-the-art sports building entitled 'The Eric Liddell Sports Centre' within the college. It was opened by double Olympic 1,500m gold medallist, Sebastian Coe. At the entrance to the centre stands a bronze figure described as 'Eric Liddell, Sportsman and Evangelist'.

Eric would not have placed much weight at all on any praise lavished on him. It would have embarrassed him. He may have smiled at what he would consider the absurdity of it all. He saw himself responsible to His Master to use what gifts and abilities had been given him. But he fully realised the Bible truth, which would have been his reply to those who wished to praise him for what they thought his achievements: 'who makes you differ *from another?* And what do you have that you did not receive? Now if you did indeed receive *it,* why do you boast as if you had not received *it?*' (1 Corinthians 4:7).

Often Eric was asked the secret of his success in sport. He once answered:

'Why, it's the three sevens!'

The 'three sevens' referred to the seventh verse of the seventh chapter of the seventh book of the New Testament. That referred to the first letter of Paul to the Corinthians, chapter 7 and verse 7:

'. . . each one has his own gift from God, one in this manner and another in that.'

It was typical of the man. He sought no praise from men. And yet, 'he being dead, yet speaketh' (Hebrews 11:4). By his worthy example of faithfulness to Christ and truth he speaks to succeeding generations, calling them to follow Christ as he did faithfully in his day.

A Final Testimony

Eric Liddell's life has had a strong influence on many people, young and old, over the years.

His life remains a fine example of a man whose life was good in the best sense. He was a man who used what talents he had to the full in a selfless way, always thinking of what service he could be to others for the Lord. He is an example of the power of faithfulness to touch the hearts and lives of others. In his athletics and in his studies and in his evangelism and in his missionary service and in his family life, his desire was to honour Christ. This was his chief end. It is in this that he speaks to succeeding generations of young and old alike.

The present writer was stirred in his heart as a nineteen-year-old to seek the Lord after reading the booklet written by D. P. Thomson. I was a keen sportsman with admittedly limited abilities. Eric's stand for the Lord's Day and willingness to turn his back on fame and fortune and devote himself to missionary service was a deeply impressive witness. It led to a re-evaluation of my life and what was really important and of eternal significance. It led to a reassessment of my relationship to God and the claims of the Lord Jesus Christ in my life. This led to coming to faith in Jesus as Saviour under the hearing of the faithful preaching of the Word. It was indirectly related to the influence of the life and witness of Eric Liddell. I never did compete again in sports on the Lord's Day, and I committed my life to the Lord, as Eric did in his day.

The question of Lord's Day observance is an issue today. The principle is the same: the first day of the week is a Lord's Day, the Christian Sabbath. It is a day for Him, for our good, for worship and for physical rest. Keeping it well is a vital testimony for a Christian believer. As much as anything it tells the world that he or she will obey God rather than men, whatever the cost. No doubt the cost will be great today for a young Christian involved in sports. There is so much Sunday sport and it is difficult to be involved in organised sport without confronting this issue. Yet the issue is to be confronted and Christians and churches should be concerned to discourage a careless use of Sundays for our own pleasures, sports, entertainments and not God's glory.

The story of Eric Liddell comes down to us over the years with a message. It is a call to faith and devotion on the one hand. It is also an encouragement of hope. His passing was felt to be a great loss by many. With some truth, the credits of the film *Chariots of Fire* announced that 'All of Scotland mourned'. Yet we are reminded that whether we are spared a short time or a long time in this life, the important thing is to be prepared for that day when we will be called out of this life. All that will count then is whether we have true faith in Christ as Saviour.

'Therefore we also, since we are surrounded by so great a cloud of witnesses, let us lay aside every weight, and the sin which so easily ensnares us, and let us run with endurance the race that is set before us, looking unto Jesus, the author and finisher of our faith, who for the joy that was set before him endured the cross, despising the shame, and has sat down at the right hand of the throne of God' (Hebrews 12:1-2).

Thinking Further Topics

Questions for Individuals and Groups

Chapter 1: Paris, 1924
Eric made an important decision about whether or not to compete in sport on Sundays. What decision did he make? How did he come to that decision? How would you feel about making a decision which might be unpopular with others?

Chapter 2: Early Years
Eric's parents and their friends faced real danger from people who might wish to harm them. How does John's gospel, chapter 16, verse 33, help the Christian deal with dangers for their faith?

Chapter 3: Family Roots
Eric was part of a Christian family. What influence would that have had on him? How is it a blessing to be brought up in a Christian home? How did Eric's father seek guidance in considering the mission field? How does Psalm 119, verses 105 to 112 help in such guidance?

Chapter 4: School Days
Life at school was not easy for Eric, being so far away from his parents. What helped him to cope? How important is

the family unit? How important is it to God? See Psalm 68, verse 6.

Chapter 5: Scholar and Sportsman

At first Eric was not keen to play sports at University. How did he come to change his mind? Are there dangers for a Christian in becoming too involved in sports?

Chapter 6: Track Champion and Evangelist

How was Eric challenged about taking a stand for Jesus? Was it easy for him to speak about his faith? Romans, chapter 10 and verse 9 teaches that if a person confesses Christ with their mouth and believes in their heart that He was raised from the dead, they will be saved. The verse teaches that with the heart one believes and with the mouth confessing Jesus as Saviour is made.

Chapter 7: A Question of Conscience

Some people might have thought that Eric was letting his country down when he refused to take part in events at the Olympic Games in 1924. Why did Eric not compete in sports on Sunday? Why is this not to be seen as letting the nation down? Acts chapter 5 and verse 29 helps us to understand Eric's position.

Chapter 8: Olympic Games Beckon

Eric was concerned in his life to honour Jesus. Why did he not pray that he would win races? Would you pray to win sports events? Read the first letter of Paul to the Corinthians, chapter 10 and verse 31 and think of how that applies to taking part in sports.

Chapter 9: 'He ran like a man inspired'

Eric's win in the Olympic 400 metres race was unexpected. How would you say that the Bible verse on the note given to him before the race helped his running that day? Eric was a modest man. Do you find it hard to be modest when you win something?

Chapter 10: Acclaim and Graduation

Eric was successful in sports and in his studies. It must have been a struggle sometimes managing both these things together. How would you set your priorities? Why is preparing for life's work more important than sports or entertainments?

Chapter 11: More Great Running

As a Christian speaker Eric often gave addresses at meetings arranged in places where he took part in sports meetings. Why was Ecclesiastes chapter 12 and verse 1 an appropriate verse to speak on with young people? Why should you remember your creator in your youth?

Chapter 12: A Year's Campaigning

Eric attended a Bible College for a year before he started missionary work. How was the experience of that year helpful and important for his future service?

Chapter 13: 'For China Now'

Eric showed dedication in his preparations for missionary work. What desire do you have to serve the Lord? How much dedication do you show in your life for Jesus?

Chapter 14: An Adventurous Journey

In going to China Eric faced uncertainties. Do uncertainties in your life make you feel worried? How would you deal with difficulties faced at home or in school? Read Psalm 55, verse 22 and Philippians 4, verses 6 and 7 for help in dealing with worries.

Chapter 15: New Beginning

In the College where Eric taught in China, there was an encouragement of Christian devotion. What habits of devotion did Eric encourage in the pupils? How did he show a good example? Do you show an example of Bible reading and prayer and Church attendance?

Chapter 16: Running Missionary

Eric continued to run in China. Why was he not tempted to try to run again in the Olympics? Read Matthew chapter 6, verse 20. How does that verse get things in the right place in our lives?

Chapter 17: Love and Marriage

Eric was married in 1934. Why should people get married? Is it just a human arrangement? What does the Bible say? See Genesis chapter 2. verse 24, together with Matthew chapter 19 and verses 1 to 10 for help.

Chapter 18: Change of Direction

It was said that Eric's secret was the practice of the presence of God. How does a person practice the presence of God? There are several things in this chapter which suggest an answer to that question. What are they?

Chapter 19: Experiences in the Country Areas

When Eric went to the country for preaching and church work, he often faced very dangerous situations. Why was he prepared to face these? Read Psalm 46 and see how the writer could face dangers confidently.

Chapter 20: Dangers of War

Eric and his family had an eventful journey to Canada during the war. What is the best thing to do when you are scared? Are such things a test of having real faith in God?

Chapter 21: Closing Scenes of Missionary Service

It was difficult for Eric to be parted from his wife and family when the situation in China became more dangerous. How did Eric use his time? Do you think on how best you can help others in your life?

Chapter 22: Captivity

There were many Christian missionaries in the Japanese prison camp. Was the presence of so many Christians a help in the ordering of the camp? How did Eric continue to encourage others to follow Christ?

Chapter 23: Home Straight

Eric passed away in the Japanese prison camp. War is a cruel thing for all who are affected by it. But how does a Christian have hope for what is beyond death? What does Matthew chapter 25, verses 31 to 46 teach us about death for the Christian and the non-Christian?

Chapter 24: Sweet Sorrow

Why was Eric called 'Mr Greatheart'? It is always sad when a loved one passes away, especially if they are young. How does the first letter to the Thessalonians chapter 4 and verse 13 encourage us concerning those who died believing in Jesus?

Chapter 25: A Grim Outcome?

There are many things that might tend to discourage Christians in Christian work in the world. How does Isaiah chapter 55 and verses 10 and 11 encourage the Christian when things seem dark in the service for the Lord Jesus?

Chapter 26: A Life Well Remembered

Eric was remembered in many ways after his passing as a fine Christian and an outstanding sportsman. How would you wish to be remembered? How can a committed Christian be a challenge to others even after their death?

Eric Liddell Timeline

1902   Eric Henry Liddell was born on 16 January, 1902 in Tientsin.

1914   First World War begins.

1920   Republic of Ireland gains independence.

1920s   Eric Liddell rose to the very heights of acclaim as an international athlete and rugby player.

1921   Insulin discovery announced.

1923   On 6 April, in a small town hall in Armadale, Scotland, Eric Liddell spoke for the first time of his faith in Christ.

1924   On Friday, 11 July, Eric Liddell won the 400m Olympic Gold medal in Paris.

1924   Eric Liddell graduated from Edinburgh University with a science degree.

1925   Eric Liddell began educational missionary work with the London Missionary Society, the Anglo-Chinese College in Tientsin, North China.

1926   First public demonstration of television by John Logie Baird.

1932   On Wednesday, 22 July, Eric was ordained to the ministry of the Scottish Congregational Church.

1933   ICI scientists discover polythene.

1934   On Tuesday, 27 March, Eric Liddell married Florence Mackenzie in Tientsin.

1935   Penguin paperbacks launched.

1937   Eric Liddell was transferred to Church-based ministry around Siaochang, North China.

1939   Second World War begins.

1941	Eric Liddell sent his wife, Florence and two children to safety in Canada when the Japanese invaded China. A third daughter was born later in the year.
1943	Eric Liddell imprisoned in a Japanese internment camp at Weihsien.
1945	On 21 February, Eric died of a brain tumour in Weihsien Internment Camp.
1952	Elizabeth II becomes Queen.
1970	First major biography of Eric Liddell, entitled *Scotland's Greatest Athlete*, written by his friend D.P. Thomson, was published in Scotland.
1973	Britain joins the European Community.
1981	The stirring account of Eric Liddell's story was made into a movie called *Chariots of Fire*.
1982	The *Chariots of Fire* movie won four 'Oscars'.
1991	On Sunday, 9 June, a Memorial Stone for Eric Liddell was dedicated on the site of the former Internment camp at Weihsien.
1994	Channel Tunnel links Britain to the European continent.
2002	Eric Liddell was one of the first 50 sportsmen and women inducted into the *Scottish Sports Hall of Fame*.
2008	On 8 August, a poll conducted by *The Scotsman* newspaper voted Eric Liddell the most popular athlete Scotland ever produced, the man who will be forever known as, 'The Flying Scotsman'.

CHINESE SPELLINGS OF
PLACE NAMES

The spelling of place names in China has varied widely over the years and has changed often. The following list shows the older spellings of place names in the first column with their pronunciations in the second column and the equivalents in the third column, as found in modern atlases.

Older place name	Pronunciation	Modern equivalent
Ch'ao Yang	chow yang	Chaoyang
Dairen	die-ren	Dalian
Peiping [Peking]	pee-king	Beijing
Pei-tai-ho	bay-du-huh	Beidaihe
Po Hai	po hi	Bo Hai
Shanghai	shang-hi	Shanghai
Shantung	shan-dung	Shandong
Siaochang	shao-chung	Zaoqiang
Taku	ta-koo	Tanggu
Tientsin	tee-in-sin	Tianjin
Tsinan	jee-nan	Jinan
Weihsien	way-shin	Weifang

The Author

John Keddie was born in Edinburgh in 1946. An athlete in his youth, he was a Scottish Junior champion in 1965 and represented Scotland on one occasion. He has long had a close interest in Eric Liddell. Learning of the story of Eric Liddell was a link in the chain, through the blessing of the Lord, by which he became a Christian in his late teens. He served as a Presbyterian minister in Morayshire (1987-1996) and on the Isle of Skye (1997-2012) up to his retirement from the pastoral ministry in April 2012. He now lives with his wife near Inverness. His acclaimed biography of Eric Liddell entitled *Running the Race: Eric Liddell, Olympic Champion and Missionary* was first published in 2007. The following year this was translated into simplified Chinese in time for the Olympic Games at Beijing.

For a full list of Trailblazers, please see our website: www.christianfocus.com All Trailblazers are available as e-books

CHRISTIAN FOCUS PUBLICATIONS

Christian Focus | Christian Heritage | CF4K | Mentor

Christian Focus Publications publishes books for adults and children under its four main imprints: Christian Focus, CF4K, Mentor and Christian Heritage. Our books reflect our conviction that God's Word is reliable and Jesus is the way to know him, and live for ever with him.

Our children's publication list includes a Sunday School curriculum that covers pre-school to early teens, and puzzle and activity books. We also publish personal and family devotional titles, biographies and inspirational stories that children will love.

If you are looking for quality Bible teaching for children then we have an excellent range of Bible stories and age-specific theological books.

From pre-school board books to teenage apologetics, we have it covered!

Find us at our web page:
www.christianfocus.com

CF4•K
Because you're never
too young to know Jesus